The Haunted Borders

Norrie McLeish

© 2010 by the author of this book Norrie McLeish retains sole copyright to his or her contributions to this book.

ISBN NO. 978-1-873708-149

Alba Publishing

Acknowledgements

This is the second edition of The Haunted Borders, which was originally published in 1997 and has been out of print, for over a decade. I have added a few more stories as well as bringing up to date some of the original ones.

Much of the research was carried out some time ago and my thanks go to the staff at the Scottish Border Archives at St Mary's Mill in Selkirk and their successors at Hawick, where the Archives are now situated. Staff at the Jedburgh Library and the National Library in Edinburgh have also been helpful.

In particular my thanks go to Hugh Mackay who tramped with me round the Borders. He has also cast his critical gaze over the early drafts of this edition and managed to identify some of my historical and grammatical errors. Thanks also to Roy Ledsham for helping to proofread the final draft.

I also have to express my thanks to Keith Robeson for allowing me to use his photo of 'The Misty Eildons' on the front cover. Keith has a wonderful range of photos of Border landscapes and they can be seen at keithrobeson.com.

Finally my thanks to my wife Isobel who has shown great patience during the long hours of research and writing.

Norrie McLeish
Jedburgh 2010

Contents

Page

3	Contents
4	Illustrations
5	Introduction
11	The Ghost of Hobkirk
19	A Legend of Tweedsmuir
27	The Lost Village
37	The Devil of Buckholm Tower
45	Merlin in The Borders
57	The Maid of Neidpath
61	Pearlin Jean
67	The Mystery of the Foul Ford
77	The Witches of Jedburgh
85	Nightmare Castle
97	The Curse of the Elliots
105	The Outlaw of Oxnam Water
113	The Ballad of Tam Lin
125	The Legend of the Linton Worm
131	A Selkirk Ghost Story
139	The Haunted Hills
147	Witchcraze in the Borders
157	The Ghosts of Littledean Tower
167	The Haunted Road
175	True Thomas
183	Index

Illustrations

Front Cover - Mist Covered Eildons
(Kind permission of Keith Robeson)

Page

10	Hobkirk Church
25	Badlieu Today
26	Tweedsmuir
36	Polwarth Kirk
44	Buckholm Tower
55	'Where Powsail meets Tweed'
56	Neidpath Tower
75	The Foul Ford
76	The Auld Brig, Jedburgh
84	Hermitage Castle
96	Site of Kidd's Tower', Liddesdale
104	Ousenam Water
124	Tam Lin's Well, Carterhaugh
138	St Mary's Kirk, Selkirk
166	Littledean Tower
174	The Benrig Road

Back Cover -
Henry Niel's monument at Foul Ford, Berwickshire.

Introduction

"The essential characteristic of a true haunt is that it is related to a place." These words were written by Andrew Lang, the Selkirk born writer, who took a great interest in supernatural matters. Most hauntings concern three types of ghostly presences; those who have died violently at a certain spot, those who have led lives of evil and decadence and finally, those who have become so attached to a particular part of this mortal world that they cannot bear to be parted from it, even after death. If this is the case, then there is scarcely a square foot of the Scottish Borderland that should not be haunted. Border history is full of places that have been the scenes of great violence that would have made many hundreds of restless spirits. For hundreds of years there were a great number of places that were identified as being haunted. A particular field or wood or hill would have had sinister associations, which were kept alive through the stories handed down from mother

to child. Sometimes the stories changed, but always the place they were associated with was regarded as being *"nae canny."* Gradually however, many of the stories were lost. Changes in the countryside saw many previously waste areas brought under cultivation. The haunted wood was razed to the ground and put under the plough and with its passing went the old stories connected with it. A deserted Borders tower succumbed to time and the weather and became a ruin. Farmers took the stones from the ruin to build houses and dykes. Soon there would be no trace of the tower. Gradually memories of those who had lived there and any stories associated with them faded from local memory.

It was not just changes in the organization of agriculture that saw a decline in the number of haunted places in the Borders. The temper of the times was changing. The growth of science and an emphasis on rationalist thought - everything must have a clear cause - together with a rejection of 'superstition' made people ashamed to say they believed in ghosts. The rhythms of life changed from those of the different seasons and the uncertain ties of nature, to one dictated by the factory bell and the office clock. Aged grandparents, whose lives were directed by an older way of doing things, became an embarrassment to their families who embraced the material benefits that the new industrial society offered them. They laughed at tales of haunted places and then forgot about them. The chain was broken and the stories disappeared.

People moved away from the places where their ancestors had lived for many generations. With their departure the association of a story with a particular place was broken. As the family settled into life in the big city or carved out a new one over the seas, a half-remembered story might be handed down that became dramatically changed in the telling. I was once contacted by an Australian family who had a tale, generations old, of how an ancestor had eloped with a Countess. The couple settled in the Australian outback where they lived happily and produced many children. I researched the tale and discovered that the young man was an agricultural labourer and the girl the daughter of a local innkeeper. They had indeed eloped to Australia. However, the social gap between them was not quite as wide as their Australian descendants had come to believe, but had become much exaggerated as the story was retold down the generations. The Borders saw many of its sons and daughters leave for much the same reasons as the Highlanders who were cleared off their ancestral lands. It was not just the people who left, with them went important parts of our Border heritage, of stories and tales many of which disappeared like fading petals blown away by a strong wind.

If many of the stories once associated with places in the Borders have disappeared it is even more the case with those stories concerning ghosts or hauntings. In the dictionary the word 'haunted' is defined as *'frequented or visited by ghosts.'* The problem is that ghosts do not appear to show themselves when you are looking for them. They come when we least expect. Even then it would appear that it is only the *'psychically sensitive'* among us who are able to detect their presence. I have been told on two occasions by people with psychic abilities that there was a presence beside me, but I was completely unaware of anything out of the ordinary - not even of a drop in temperature. I also know of people who will not go near certain places in the Borders because of the sinister atmosphere they sense. Often this is when they have no knowledge of the history of the place. I know one lady who will not go near Hermitage Castle or Littledean Tower. Perhaps after reading this book she will realise why she has avoided them.

The difficulty is that there are any number of other people who live and work close to these places who are quite unaware of and unaffected by any ghostly presences. In many cases they are unaware of the stories that surround the house next door or of the tales surrounding the ruined tower that once stood nearby. If they do become aware of them, does that mean that there will be an increase in the sightings of spectral figures? There is an old superstition that if the phantoms of the past are forgotten they will simply disappear. The question springs to mind though; if someone comes along and rediscovers old tales are the ghosts resurrected at the same time?

This is not a book about ghosts in white sheets or things that go bump in the night. In a sense we are all haunted by the memories of our past from which we cannot escape. We are haunted by the lives of our ancestors, whose genes, culture and beliefs make us who we are. So that deserted village can be haunted, at the very least, in our minds by those who used to live there and that particular stream or hill can be rich in associations with the old ones who once regarded the Borderland as theirs. By finding out about them and rediscovering their tales and the places particularly associated with them, we are, in a sense, bringing them back to haunt us. I feel this to be particularly true, when we discover our ancestor's treatment of those accused of being witches. It is more than likely that it was our ancestors who stood and jeered as a woman, half demented by torture, was burned at the stake. What black corners of the human soul are revealed in that dark episode of Borders history? Belief in witchcraft may have publicly disappeared but I fear that the mind-set from which it came is still very much alive.

Belief in ghosts and the supernatural is as old as mankind itself, only recently has a more rational view of the universe taken hold. But already scientists are challenging the mechanistic view of creation. We are unlocking the hidden areas of the mind; the power of the subconscious has long been recognized. Why is it that a flock of as many as 50,000 birds, can turn in synchrony in less than a twentieth of a second? Scientists have recorded such happenings on high-speed film. A possible explanation is that they are responding collectively to certain, as yet undetected stimuli. Science itself is approaching the boundaries between the natural world and that called the supernatural.

When all the arguments about the existence or non-existence of ghosts are exhausted, it remains the case that there are places in the Borders that have strange stories associated with them. Many of these have been lost. I hope that in this book I am able to introduce you to some forgotten tales that make up an important part of our Border heritage or let you see another aspect of a familiar Border tale.

The Haunted Borders

Hobkirk Church Today
– Nicol Edgar's church stood on the mound in the foreground

The Ghost of Hobkirk

The Reverend Nicol Edgar was appointed minister to the parish of Hobkirk in the valley of the Rule in September 1694. It must have been with some sense of misgiving that he took up his post in this poor and remote corner of the Borders. It was part of what had been a bloody and lawless frontier area before the union of the two kingdoms of Scotland and England in 1603. Here the wild Turnbull clan had held sway. The ruins of their massive peel towers stand as mute testimony to their reputation for ruthlessness and cruelty at a time when murder, rape, kidnapping and extortion were part of the very fabric of Borders society. Mounted on sturdy ponies, Turnbull shepherds wore armour and stood holding their pikes while tending their flocks, ready to defend themselves and perhaps do a little raiding of their own if the opportunity presented itself. The legacy of these centuries of bloodshed and strife was widespread poverty that helped make a dour and fiercely independent people, hardened to adversity and suspicious of outsiders. It would take many generations for the land to come to terms with the relative peace that descended on the Borders after 1603. Some Turnbulls who had successfully survived in a wild and war-torn Borderland found it impossible to acquire the different life-skills necessary to prosper in times of peace. More accustomed to the art of war than the rigours of financial management necessary in times of peace, they found themselves forced to sell off their ancestral lands, and became scattered throughout the United Kingdom and overseas.

The early Christian church must have found the Rule valley a hard soil in which to sow to sow a message of love and forgiveness. But it did try. In 1211 the monks of Jedburgh built a substantial, stone church in Hobkirk and a hospital for lepers was established nearby. The long and bloody wars of independence wiped away these indicators of a more gentle human existence. In time, a replacement church was built, but it was a poor thing compared to its predecessor, and by 1690 it had fallen into ruin and was unfit for any kind of public worship. Two years prior to this, the church in the neighbouring parish of Southdean had collapsed without warning on the Sabbath. Fortunately the congregation had just left the building before it came tumbling down; symbolic perhaps, of the tenuous hold the church had over the hearts and minds of the people of the Rule valley.

The Reverend Nicol Edgar was to inherit a new building, completed in 1692, grudgingly built by the local heritors who spent as little as possible on it. It was a very unprepossessing barn-like structure, typical of the time, with a low roof, thatched with heather and an earthen floor. It had not been built to last. In 1758 the minister stated that it was in a wretched condition. A few years later complaints were made that it was damp and dirty and that the level of the earthen floor was two feet below that of the kirkyard outside. The kirkyard itself did not reflect the picturesque scene with which we are familiar today. Sheep and cattle were allowed to pasture there, kept in only by a low stone dyke. At festival times wives sold gingerbread and sweet things, using the tops of tombstones as counters. Doubtless other transactions of a slightly less legal nature were also carried out in the kirkyard. Smuggling and illicit whisky distilling were prevalent in the parish. In 1846 workmen digging up the church floor unearthed a great quantity of human bones that had been buried just below the surface. It had been the custom, prior to the reformation, to bury the dead within the kirk itself. No doubt the health hazards created by this practice contributed to the less than average life span of the Hobkirk ministers who spent so much of their time living on top of such physical decay.

Nicol Edgar was 36 years old in 1694 and was the younger son of the Laird of Wedderlie in Berwickshire. His wife, Susannah, was the daughter of William Veitch, minister of Westruther. Her father and her uncle had both suffered persecution for their support of the Covenant and their continued resistance to the royal attempts to impose an Episcopalian system of government on the Church of Scotland. Hobkirk had been without a minister for five years prior to Nicol Edgar taking up the post. The previous minister, John Liddel, had been deposed by the Privy Council for *"not praying for their majesties, William and Mary."* He was accused of stating that, *"he would never pray for them as long as his blood was warm."*

These were bad times for Scotland. The country was only just recovering from the murderous conflict between the Covenanters and the state. The recent massacre at Glencoe had damaged the reputation of the crown and much of the land lay in the grip of a terrible and prolonged famine.

For twenty-six years Nicol Edgar toiled as the minister to the folk of Hobkirk. We know little of his ministry during these years nor of how he was regarded by the superstition-riddled people of the parish. It was the events of the year 1720 that were to make Nicol Edgar long remembered by the generations that followed.

He was then sixty-two years of age. His wife, Susannah, had died seven years earlier and his seventeen - year- old son had followed her to the grave two years later. He lived with his two young daughters, Susannah and Elizabeth. This was a time when the supernatural was part of the everyday lives of the country folk. Certain actions had to be taken to fend off evil spirits; mostly centred on the need to protect livestock and crops on which the continued existence of the community depended. Scarlet thread was wound round the horns of cattle to prevent them from being bewitched, rowan trees were planted in front of houses to ward off evil spirits. So deeply embedded were these practices that the church usually turned a blind eye except where local tensions led to an outbreak of witch persecution. There is no evidence of such persecutions breaking out in Hobkirk. We do not know if Nicol Edgar shared the beliefs of his parishioners. Perhaps his living among them for so long in such an isolated parish, gradually led him to absorb the customs and habits of his flock, most of which his church regarded as dangerous and ungodly.

In 1720 a kind of mass hysteria gripped the people of Hobkirk. The ghost of a tall man with a blue bonnet had been seen prowling among the tombstones of the kirkyard. It was even said to have sat in the pews of the kirk during divine service, causing several women to have attacks of nervous hysterics. Whether this was an unconscious device to break the monotony of the long sermons characteristic of the time is a moot point. Apparently prayers were ineffective in ridding the community of this restless spirit. It was not, however, until his own daughters refused to venture out after dark for fear of the ghost, that the Reverend Edgar decided that it was time to take action. Armed with the kirk bible and an old claymore, a family heirloom, he set off at night for the kirk. The claymore was probably made of iron, a metal believed to be feared by witches and other creatures of the supernatural. He entered the church and drew a circle with his claymore in the earth around the pulpit. He then sat down inside the circle to await events.

His long vigil lasted throughout the night. In the hour before dawn he heard a strange noise coming from the eastern corner of the church. An eerie light spread out from the corner, and the astonished minister observed an upheaval in the earth that slowly grew to the size of a small hillock. The figure of a man emerged, wearing a blue bonnet and dressed, as was the fashion of the time, in breeches and blue stockings. The apparition fixed his eyes on the minister and strode towards him. It stopped at the circle then proceeded to remove its blue stockings and casually tossed them over the pew in front of the pulpit. Carefully the minister leaned over and picked up one of the stockings with the point of his sword. On examining them, he found that they were made of ordinary homespun yarn. Although a chill swept through the minister, the everyday nature of the garment also gave him confidence and he demanded of the spirit why he was causing such terror among the people of the parish. The ghost replied that he had been a cattle dealer who had been robbed and murdered on the moors nearby when making his way home from Lammas Fair. He claimed that his spirit would find no rest until his murderers had been found. After a while the minister was able to persuade the ghost to restrict his nocturnal wanderings to a more remote part of the parish. The ghost vanished never to be seen again and the Reverend Nicol Edgar emerged from the church, no doubt thoroughly shaken by his ordeal.

Such is the story that became part of the folklore of this little Borders parish and, no doubt it became embellished in the telling and retelling. It does contain elements that are more commonly found in Highland stories of the supernatural. Hillocks were regarded as entrances to and exits from the 'Otherworld' where dwelt the spirits of the dead. Iron or steel was seen as an effective safeguard against evil spirits. Even more common was the belief that the living had to be protected against the spirits of those who had died before their time. All of those elements together with use of the protective circle are present in this tale, indicative perhaps of how firmly the old Celtic superstitions still held sway in the minds of people. Even more telling is that those who were able to converse with the spirits of the 'Otherworld' were regarded as being in possession of the *'second sight.'* Those who possessed this ability were regarded with dread and suspicion by their fellow-beings. Such was the fate of the Reverend Nicol Edgar. Far from being grateful to the minister for ridding them of the troublesome spirit, they regarded him as being *'no canny'* - a view that was to continue even after his death.

Nicol Edgar died four years after his confrontation with the ghost of the cattle dealer in the church of Hobkirk. But there was a real fear among the local folk that his *uncanny* spirit would return to haunt them. It was decided that his body should be dug up and taken to a more remote place. In the dead of night a group of villagers proceeded to dig up the minister's corpse and binding it up with ropes, they started to carry it off with the intention of re-burying it some distance from the village. As they approached the foot of Bonchester Hill one of the party stumbled. An arm of the corpse came loose and struck one of the men carrying it in the face. This was too much for the already nervous group. They dropped the body and fled in terror. The body of the minister lay out all that night and it was not recovered until the next day when it was taken back and re-interred in the kirkyard. The stone above the grave was inscribed: *Here lys Nicol Edgar, son of the Laird of Wedderlie, who died upon the 31st of May 1724 aged 67 years. And his spouse Susanna, who died 30th June 1713, aged 52.*

The old church was taken down in 1852 and a much more imposing edifice was erected in its place. With its removal the story of Nicol Edgar and his encounter with the world of the supernatural began to fade from local memory as the valley of the Rule Water adjusted to the demands of a more rational age.

Getting There

Hobkirk is about 8 miles south east of Hawick. You take the

A6088 to Bonchester Bridge. On entering the village, you turn right, it will be signposted for Hobkirk. The present Hobkirk Church is an imposing Victorian building, on the right hand side of the road. As you go through the gate, you will see a mound in front of you and slightly to the right. This is where the Rev. Nicol Edgar's church stood and where he had the confrontation that was to become the stuff of Borders' legend.

A Legend of Tweedsmuir

A hundred thousand years is no more than the blink of an eye in geological time. But looking back to try and uncover events in Scotland a thousand years ago is like trying to peer through dense fog that thickens as we travel further back into the past. We glimpse shadows that appear briefly and then disappear. There are some historical records that were written up by mostly Irish monks and were concerned in the main, with royal dynasties and battles. Often they contradict each other or leave frustrating gaps in the narrative. Archaeology is uncovering more information and as analytical techniques improve, we will no doubt uncover more of what is often referred to as *"dark age Scotland"*.

Another important source of history is that of oral tradition. Scotland was a mostly pre-literate society until the early 19th century. Before this local history and stories were passed on by word of mouth over many generations. Often the stories changed in the telling, as all stories do, and sometimes they were retold within a different setting. The tale would have been passed from one locality and set in another. Sometimes as a story became less relevant to the audience it gradually disappeared and was lost to history. But occasionally a tale resonated down the centuries and was repeated at a hearthside for generation after generation. Where the story was localised, it seldom travelled further than the area in which the story was set. Such a tale is the story of love and tragedy that is firmly placed in Badlieu in the wild and fairly empty landscape of Tweedsmuir.

In 1799 the parish minister of Tweedsmuir described his parish as being, *"distinguished by the bleakness and moorishness of its aspect."* It is a description that can still fit on dull, autumn Scottish mornings. It is wild and hilly with its highest peaks at Hart Fell and Broadlaw rising to over 2000 feet. Here we find the source of the river Tweed, rising sluggishly in the foothills until it is quickly fed by the Core, Fruid and Talla burns and then it is rapidly transformed into the iconic Border river that makes its stately way to Berwick-upon-Tweed and the sea. It is now a sparsely populated area but the remains of hill forts and other bronze and iron age sites suggest that at one time the population was much more numerous.

Much later, by the end of the 10th century a large part of Tweedsmuir was a royal hunting forest. A forest was not necessarily made up of dense woodland but could mean that it was wasteland usually with some woods and scrubland. Much of Scotland at this time was still covered in such woods and scrubland, with bogs and morasses in low-lying areas. The forests of Tweedsmuir were greatly favoured by the early kings of Scotland and when they were not defending their realm against challengers to their throne or repelling Norse invaders, they spent their leisure hours hunting.

Sometime before 1000 the king of Alba was Kenneth, the son of Duff. He is sometimes referred to as *'Kenneth the Grim'*, but this seems to have been a mistranslation and it is more likely to have been *'Kenneth the brown haired one'*. He was the third Kenneth to have reigned and he acquired his throne by defeating and killing his predecessor Constantine in the year 995. This seemed to be the way of these early Scottish/Pictish kings. The throne did not pass from father to son automatically, but usually went to a relative who was an adult and who seemed capable of defending his kingdom. This was particularly important as Scotland was being subjected to continuous harassments from the Norsemen whose early raiding had developed into capturing land for settlement and colonisation. Unfortunately the system often meant that there were continual challenges to the king by hopeful and ambitious relatives. Few of these early kings died peacefully in their beds.

The centre of royal activity at this time was in Fortrui in northern Perthshire; for this was the time when the Scots and the Picts became united under one ruler, a necessary first step on the road to what was to become Scotland. It is not clear whether Kenneth was more Pict than Scot, but what we do know is that Tweedsmuir was a great distance from his ancestral lands. Not only that but it was part of the kingdom of Strathclyde which was a kingdom in its own right separate from the new united land of Scot and Pict that was referred to as Alba. But it was a very fluid situation. Sometimes kings of Strathclyde recognized the kings of Alba as their overlords and at others times they were totally independent. While the military and political changes in the Tweed valley of the 10th century are obscure, we can get a clue from the place names of the area. It is significant that Badlieu just north of the source of the river Tweed is derived from the Celtic; *"am bad fliuch"* - meaning *"spot of wetness"*. It is of Gaelic origin and not of Brythonnic Welsh, that would have been the language of the Britons of Strathclyde. This is perhaps an indicator of how far the Scots language had penetrated the Tweed valley.

Whatever the subsequent history showed, at the end of the 10th century Kenneth III was king of Alba and enjoyed hunting in Tweedsmuir, which was part of the vast Wood of Caledon with thickets of hazel and birch. Kenneth was the son of a previous king called Duff who was violently murdered. In 995 Kenneth defeated the reigning king, Constantine, in a battle near the mouth of the river Almond in Perthshire. Constantine was killed and Kenneth took the throne. He was to reign for eight years and was generally regarded as an able and fair king. Though what was judged as *"able and fair"* in 10th century Scotland would be very different from our 21st century ideas. Other than this we know very little about about Kenneth III.

Local tradition says that Kenneth was at Polmood, the royal hunting lodge, in the autumn. Somehow he had managed to get separated from the main hunting party and got lost as the evening mist descended. He found himself in what was marshland when he saw a light from a shepherd's cottage halfway up the nearby hillside. He made his way towards it and was greeted by the herd's daughter. Now any semi-attractive daughter of a peasant would have been regarded as fair game by male members of the nobility and the king would have expected no resistance if he were so inclined. The girl's name was Bertha and it was not long before she was installed in Polmood Lodge as the king's mistress. It soon became clear to members of the court that this was no ordinary affair and that the king was totally besotted by the young shepherd's daughter. Kenneth had a wife and family and while no doubt, faithfulness in marriage was not considered a virtue, however where a mistress or concubine had aspirations above her station then things got difficult. No doubt Kenneth's queen and her advisors became alarmed at the amount of time he was spending at Polmood Lodge. Their alarm would have increased when Bertha gave birth to a son. Along with her natural resentment and jealousy, the queen and her advisors saw a new danger, a possible future claimant to the throne. Bertha and her newborn son had now become a problem.

There had been a major invasion by Vikings in the north and Kenneth had to raise an army to repel them. He marched north and inflicted a resounding defeat on the invading force. He returned to Fortrui where he had to deal with the aftermath of victory and also to be there with his queen who had succumbed to what was to be a fatal illness. She died and immediately he headed south for Polmood and Badlieu.

We do not know if he had any foreknowledge of what he would find there. Perhaps his eagerness to believe that all was well there overcame any concerns he may have had for the safety of Bertha and his child. When he arrived, it was to meet a scene of devastation. Badlieu had been ransacked and there was no sign of Bertha, their child and her father. Soon some of the local peasantry began to appear and with some nervousness, they told the warrior king what had happened. The queen had sent a band of assassins to murder Bertha and her child. They had killed them along with her old father and buried their bodies on the hillside above Badlieu. Kenneth was distraught with grief. He had their bodies uncovered so he could be sure that it was true.

It is said that he never recovered from his grief over the death of Bertha and his child. His interest in ruling the kingdom waned. In 1013 he was challenged by his cousin Malcolm for the throne and was defeated and killed at Monivaird in Perthshire. He was buried in Iona, the traditional resting place of Scottish kings.

As was the custom, the male relatives of Kenneth were hunted down and killed by Malcolm, in order to prevent any challenges to his rule. But, he had a granddaughter, Gruoch, who took as her second husband Macbeth, then Mormaer of Moray. Macbeth defeated Duncan, Malcolm's grandson, and took the throne of Scotland. Gruoch, of course, is remembered as the wife who drove her husband to kill and seize the throne in Shakespeare's 'Macbeth'.

It is still a lonely spot, Badlieu, set on a hillside in the Tweedsmuir valley. The great Wood of Caledon has long been stripped of its trees and most of the land is moorland and in the low-lying area around the source of the Tweed, still marshy. Locals used to say that in autumn when the mists gather and the wind gets up, the ghosts of Bertha and her murdered child can be seen blown like wisps of fog and nearby searching for them but not seeing them is the grim form of a heartbroken and despairing Kenneth III.

Getting There

From Selkirk take the A708 towards Moffat. Before Moffat turn up the A701 on your left. A few miles on you will see on your right a sculpting marking Tweed's Well, the source of the Tweed. About two miles further on, on the right is the farm of Badlieu. This is the area where Bertha lived and died.

Badlieu Today

Tweedsmuir today, looking north from Tweed's Well. The white cottage stands near where Bertha's cottage would have been situated

The Lost Village

There is a forgotten corner of Berwickshire that has long held a romantic and significant place in Scotland's history. Poets have praised the village of Polwarth's beauty; it has provided a haven for the persecuted and was the setting for a story of courage that is now part of our national folklore, as well as being the home of prominent statesmen. But Polwarth's glories are now in the past. All that remains of this ancient village are a few crumbling remains of ruined cottages in an overgrown field, and soon even these will be gone. Stand there for a few moments, though, on a warm summer's evening. Soon the faint sounds of a fiddle can be heard, children laugh, anxious mothers call them home and the village comes to life. But it only lasts a moment and we are left standing with only the gathering breeze to keep us company.

Polwarth is an ancient place. Its first church was dedicated to St Kentigern (or St Mungo) who died in 603 AD. It was probably built on a site that had been a pagan place of worship as was the practice of the Christian missionaries. Gaelic and Saxon influences are reflected in the name, derived from the Gaelic 'pol', a marshy place and the Saxon 'worth', meaning a settlement.

Little is known of Polwarth's very early history but it must have been a place of some importance as it held St Mungo's Fair twice a year. Horses and cattle were traded on the first day, the second being devoted to more general merchandise. Polwarth would also have been a frequent victim of the long wars with England, but the village's no doubt harrowing experiences during those turbulent times have not been recorded

The Polwarth family is first mentioned in a charter issued in the reign of Alexander II (1214-1249). They would probably have adopted their surname from the lands they held. The line died out and Polwarth passed to the Sinclairs through marriage. Several generations later, the Humes acquired it, once again through marriage. Recently the McEwan family owned the estate until it was sold off.

The manner in which the Humes managed to make Polwarth part of their own lands created a romantic tradition that was to make Polwarth famous throughout the land. Sir Patrick de Polwarth died in the late 14th century leaving his only child, a daughter Elizabeth, as his sole heir. She married Sir John Sinclair of Herdmanston. Their great-grandson died without male issue, and the heirs to his estate were his daughters, Marion and Margaret. Not surprisingly the youthful heiresses soon attracted the attentions of the young lairds of the district. George and Patrick Hume of Wedderburn were looked upon with the greatest favour by Marion and Margaret.

This displeased the girls' uncle, Sir William Sinclair. If the girls died as spinsters, he would become sole heir to their estates.

He refused to give the girls permission to marry and promptly imprisoned them in his tower on the far side of the Lammermuirs. For months the Hume brothers searched for them, but eventually Marion and Margaret managed to get word to them through an old beggar woman. The suitors, at the head of a band of horsemen, rode to Herdmanston, successfully besieged it, and carried their lady loves back to Polwarth to be wed.

As part of the celebrations, the marriage dance took place around an ancient thorn tree growing in the centre of the village green. Thus began the custom by which every village wedding included a dance around the thorn tree. The tradition became the subject of many songs and poems, the best known by Alan Ramsay:

At Polwarth on the green
If you'll meet me on the morn
Where lasses do convene
To dance about the thorn

The first two lines are taken from a much older poem, which reads:

At Polwarth on the green
If you'll meet me on the morn
Our forebears oft were seen
To dance about the thorn
When they got in their corn

It may well be that the custom of dancing round the thorn to celebrate harvest had links with ancient pagan traditions, the origins of which have long been lost and which were far older than that first marriage ceremony. The Polwarth minister, writing at the end of the 18th century noted in referring to the custom of dancing around the thorn tree *'This custom has fallen much into disuse, there not having been above two instances of it these twenty years.'* In 1835, a wedding party danced around the descendant of the original thorn, but only after persuading an old woman to show them the steps of the dance.

Polwarth Kirk stands slightly above the village to the south-east, at the top of the brae. Legend has it that two packmen quarrelled at St Mungos Fair, as a result of which one was killed. The victim was buried where he was struck down and the hillside between the village and the church has been known as Packman's Brae ever since. A stone is said to have marked the site of his grave. The church was extensively rebuilt in 1703, but according to the inscription above the door, it was consecrated in the year 900, though there has probably been a church here since 600. It was rededicated in 1242 and then fell into ruin until it was rescued by Sir John Sinclair about 1578. In 1703 the church was rebuilt with the addition of a bell-tower. It has hardly changed since then.

The churchyard was the setting for a tale of heroism that has become part of the folklore of Scotland. Sir Patrick Hume, born in 1641, was a staunch Presbyterian. So outspoken was he that he was declared by the authorities to be a 'fractious person. In despair, he planned to leave the country and set up a Presbyterian settlement in North Carolina, a project that had received the approval of the King. Unfortunately, some of Sir Patrick's friends and co-planners were accused of being involved in a plot to kill the Duke of York. A close friend of Sir Patrick, Baillie of Jerviswoode, was arrested and subsequently executed. Although Sir Patrick maintained his innocence, the authorities determined on his arrest and he had to go into hiding. He took refuge in the vault of Polwarth Kirk, about a mile from his home in Redbraes Castle, while soldiers scoured the countryside for him. The vault was very narrow with only a chink of light coming through a narrow slit at the end. Every night his young daughter, Grizell, would bring him food and drink. To do so, she had to overcome her fear of the dark and of the dangers presented by the searching soldiers, for only she and her mother knew where her father was hidden. To avoid suspicion she slipped food off her own plate to take to him. At the supper table one evening her younger brother almost gave the game away when he exclaimed, *"Mother, will ye look at Grizell: while we have been eating our broth, she has eaten up the whole sheep's-heid!"*

After a month, the search for Sir Patrick died down and it was considered safe for him to return home. He moved to a room on the ground floor and a hole was dug as a hiding place from unwelcome visitors. Bed and blankets were placed in it, in case his stay had to be extended. Dampness, however, was a constant worry as Redbraes had been built on very boggy ground. One morning, the floor boards were lifted and the bed shot out having been pushed to the top by water flooding the hole.

Sir Patrick decided to tempt providence no further and fled to The Netherlands with his family. He lived there in relative poverty until his return to Scotland in 1688 after 'The Glorious Revolution' that brought William of Orange to Britain. His estates were restored to him and he rose rapidly in the King's esteem, becoming a member of the Privy Council and later a peer of the realm as Lord Polwarth and Earl of Marchmont. He died in 1724. Grizell, his brave young daughter, married an old friend and became Lady Grizell Baillie. She had a long life and was to become a poet of some distinction. The original Redbraes Tower, built by the first Lords of Polwarth, has disappeared. The second has also gone, but the remains of the third castle are incorporated into the service areas of the present Marchmont House, which was built about 1754. Constructed in the semi-Palladian style, and surrounded by gardens, it was for a while a centre for the Sue Ryder Foundation, helping disabled people. There are currently plans to restore it to a private residence.

Polwarth village became a refuge for Huguenots fleeing from France after the revocation of the Edict of Nantes that sparked off a period of severe persecution for French Protestants. They landed at Berwick-upon-Tweed and some made their way inland with many of them settling in the village of Polwarth. The fugitives brought with them many skills including working with leather and an expertise in building. Only the sites of the old tan pits remain in the woods around Polwarth today, but Polwarth is still remembered as a *'village of shoemakers'*. Many of the farmhouses and mansions in the district were built by descendants of the Huguenot *'asylum seekers'*.

The village was built on wet and swampy ground with the houses scattered haphazardly around the green. The minister, writing for the statistical account in 1793, observed that almost every home had a hole dug to collect water that had to be emptied after spells of wet weather. Despite this, it would appear that epidemics were few and there are reports of some people living to a considerable old age. The same minister emphasised the low rents charged by the Earl of Marchmont, but commented on the number of old and infirm who were employed by the Earl *"for work they were not able to perform."* Writing in 1834, the minister of that time recorded, *"All the poor in the parish have a free house and garden through the benevolence of Sir W.P.M Campbell of Marchmont."*

No doubt it was this paternalistic care that made many Polwarth folk reluctant to move away from the village. A report prepared for the Earl in 1819 stated: *"The village of Polwarth has been a considerable burden upon the estate, from the expense of maintaining indigent persons, the low rate at which the land was formerly leased out for the encouragement of the inhabitants, and the expenses of keeping the various cottages in repair."*

For many years the village was a self-sustaining unit, far from the developing towns and cities. In 1791 there were three wrights, a mason, a smith, two weavers, two tailors, five shoemakers, a tanner and three carters. The village was well-known for the skill of its shoemakers, many of them descended from Huguenot refugees. Polwarth fiddlers were always in demand at local weddings and harvest kirns. In 1826 there was a schoolmaster, as well as two grocers and a joiner living in the village. It all suggests a thriving community, fairly content and not keen on venturing very far afield. A common saying in Berwickshire was, *"Polwarth folk winna marry oot o their ain parish."*

The late Madge Elder could remember her mother, born in Polwarth, telling her about some of the characters in the village, such as George Calder, the baker, who always wore a *'lum hat'* even in the bakehouse. The red glow of the ovens, seen through the open door, combined with the shadow of the baker with the hat, fascinated the young village children. She also remembered the story of an old woman who went out to milk her cow, pastured in a field near the village. Eventually, they found her sitting on a bank, milk pail by her side and her feet in the burn. She told them that on her way home, some fairies had cast a spell on her. After dancing around her and laughing they had made off. When they had gone she found that she could not move and had to sit until someone came to help her.

Robert McLean Calder, was the son of George Calder, the Polwarth baker. Born and raised in Polwarth he later lived and worked in Canada and the United States, but never lost his love for his native village. His *'Memories of Polwarth'*, as well as reflecting his own feelings, gives us an insight into life in the village in the middle of the 19th century. He recalls the gathering of worthies at the door of the smiddy, resolving the questions of the day, gossiping and teasing the lasses. He remembers dancing to the music of the fiddle at Hogmanay, harvest kirns, *'the auld scbule house on the green'* and sitting in the ingle neuk around a blazing peat fire, listening to stories of *'ghaists and bogles.'* His is undoubtedly a romantic view, coloured by nostalgia for a lifestyle that was already passing away. On his frequent trips home, he observed the steady deterioration of the village; the houses, barns and mill declining. He had no doubts as to why this was happening:

the auld shamefu story
O a near or graspin laird.

The increasing commercial pressure on land usage was undoubtedly a factor in the decline of Polwarth. The old 'fermtouns' were breaking up. New social and financial relationships between landowner and tenant farmer and worker were being established. An improving communications network, the growing attractions of towns and cities, all served to break down the previous isolation of rural communities. As early as 1852 the Berwickshire Naturalists' Society noted: *"... and so we passed to Polwarth.. The poor houses - the undrained common - did no credit to the lord of the manor. We saw nothing on our walk from Polwarth to the church but a manse out of place, and out of proportion to the living. The common green at Polwarth is capable of being made ornamental; but the pigs and geese have unstinted privilege over it, along with the donkey; and it is uncomfortable and rough from lack of drainage."*

After the Great War the population diminished rapidly and by the 1950s village was deserted. But if you stand by the old thorns at dusk on a summer evening with the breeze rustling through the leaves, you may just hear the sound of the fiddle, the boisterous laughter of the men and the giggles of the lasses and weans playing wi muckle din:

The wedding Johns adjourn,
An march wi fiddler at thir heid
To dance aroun' the thorn.
I only wish they still did.

Getting There

Polwarth is just over 3 miles from Duns. Take the A6105 road from Duns to Greenlaw and you will see the sign for Polwarth on your left-hand side. Turn right down a little sidetrack and after a few yards you will see a gate. This gate opens up to a small bridge that leads you into the site of the main part of Polwarth village. The site has been purchased with a view to building luxury houses and at the moment the village green is much like a building site.

Thankfully, a condition of planning is that the old thorn tree with its protective rail should be preserved. It is much overgrown, with thistles and nettles very prevalent. It would be nice to think that Polwarth could once again resound with the sound of new life even if it is the noise of lawnmowers, cars being washed and gardens being sprinkled. To get to the church go back on to the road and go up the Packman's Brae. The church is on the left-hand side.

Polwarth Kirk

The Devil of Buckholm Tower

There are some places, which because of their design or architectural style or perhaps as a result of their dramatic situation, actually look as if they should be haunted. Local legend often obliges with an appropriate tale. The ruins of Buckholm Tower just outside Galashiels do not seem all that different from many of the ancient keeps that are scattered throughout the Borders. They differ, however, by the fact that strange and terrible stories have long been associated with these old ruins and it was the scene of the last recorded 'laying' of an evil spirit by an ordained minister of the Church of Scotland.

Originally known as Bucklem Tower, it was built about the middle of the 16th century when it was the property of the Hop-Pringles, who later were to drop the prefix 'Hop'. It was as the Pringles that the clan was to become one of the foremost of the great robber

The Haunted Borders

or reiving families of the Scottish middle march. The Pringles were wild men, well suited for the wild times of the 16th century Borderland. The lairds of Buckholm were as wild and lawless as any of their cousins. It is recorded that in 1570, Johne Hop-Pringle of Buckholm together with his kinsmen in Torwoodlee, Blyndley and Galashiels were obliged by the Regent Murray to find security for their good behaviour. In 1591 James Hop-Pringle was put under caution to the extent of £2000 to keep the peace. Lack of respect for the law seems to have paid off for the Pringles, as it did for other Border families, for at one time practically the whole of the valley of the Gala was in the hands of the family.

No doubt the old stones of Buckholm Tower are silent witnesses to a great deal of atrocious behaviour and in this they would have been no different from those of many another border tower. After 1603, however, the days of reiving and blood feud gradually came to an end. Not that Scotland and the Borders were to enjoy peace and prosperity for some time yet. Scotland in the 17th century was a land riven by dissent and civil war and the Borders was to suffer accordingly. It was from this period that Buckholm Tower was to acquire its evil reputation.

The restoration of Charles II to the throne in 1660 brought about an end to Britain's flirtation with republicanism but it did not bring an end to the religious strife that beset Scotland. The religious ideas of the reformation settlement were never as important to the Scottish nobility as the chance of getting their hands on the church lands. After they had got them, they tended to look to a form of church organisation in which they could play a major role and thus exercise a form of social control over the mass of the people. By and large the landowners supported an Episcopalian church structure with the monarch as the head, backed by archbishops and bishops. In particular they wanted to keep the power to appoint ministers. On the other side were those who wanted a structure where the elected Kirk Session was the focus of power in the church and their representatives formed the General Assembly. In the latter half of the 17th century those who supported the latter view were called Covenanters. The return of Charles II was to see a restoration of an Episcopal church structure. Many ministers could not accept the new structure and were replaced by more accommodating clergy many of whom were untrained. The sympathies of most people lay with the exiled ministers many of whom started to hold outdoor services called conventicles. The government regarded these as seditious and they were put down and landowners severely fined if a conventicle was held on their land. The severity and harshness of the government only succeeded in making the Covenanters more fanatical in their faith and helped create many 'martyrs' for the Covenant. This period is often referred to as the 'Killing Times' and the central Borders was one of the areas where support for the Covenanters was strong.

The Pringles were divided in their reactions to the troubles of the times. The Pringles of Torwoodlee were to remain supporters of the Covenant but George Pringle, the Laird of Buckholm, despite marrying a daughter of James Pringle of Torwoodlee, remained a committed Royalist. This was evident from an early date, for in 1646 George Pringle was called before the Selkirk Presbytery, *"to bring him to repentance for joining the rebells."* The 'rebells' were Montrose and his followers who had gone down to a bloody defeat at Philiphaugh the previous year. No doubt he laid low during the Cromwell years, but with the return of Charles II and the advent of the troubles he proved to be a fanatical enemy of the Covenant. He took part in the suppression of the Covenanters at the battle of Bothwell Bridge and indeed had to be reprimanded for his zealousness for *"setting upon John Durie of Grange thinking he was a reble."*

As he grew older it is said his cruelty increased, as did his hatred of dissenters. His wife and son left him. His son embraced the Covenanting cause with all the fervour with which his father opposed it, and was to complain to the authorities of his father *"being riotous and having imprisoned him in Melrose tolbooth."* The laird is said to have owned two ferocious hounds, which he used to hunt down Covenanters who frequently met on the wastes of Ladhope Moor. When the persecution of the Covenanters was at its height, a troop of dragoons, commanded by a Captain Bruce, arrived at Buckholm. They had got wind of a conventicle that was to be held on the moor and they had come to Pringle for advice on where to look. He, of course, was delighted to help and, accompanied by his hounds, led them on to the moor. The Covenanters though, had heard about the dragoons and had fled. One of them, an old man named Geordie Elliot, had fallen from his horse and his son, also named George, remained to try and help him. It was not long before George Pringle and the dragoons came upon them. Pringle wanted the men killed on the spot but was persuaded by Captain Bruce to take them back as prisoners to Buckholm Tower. After the dragoons had left, Pringle had the two men flung in the tower dungeon. He then sat down at his table where he ate a solitary meal and then drank himself into a morose and evil-tempered disposition. His servants frequently interrupted to tell him that young George was calling for help for his father who was in a poor condition. Pringle staggered downstairs, went inside the dungeon and closed the door behind him. The servants listened fearfully to the sounds of raised voices and heavy blows followed by a dragging noise and muted screams. The screams went on for some time to be followed by an ominous silence. Eventually the laird emerged, wild eyed, dishevelled and cursing. He locked the dungeon door behind him and forbade his servants to go near it.

He returned to his table and continued to drink. The atmosphere among the servants in the tower was muted and fearful. There was a knocking at the door. A servant came up and tremblingly told the laird that old Isobel Elliot, the wife and mother of the prisoners, was at the door looking for her husband and son. With a roar of drunken rage, Pringle got up, lurched downstairs and grabbed hold of the old woman. He took her down to the dungeon, opened the door and ushered her drunkenly inside. As the old woman's eyes became accustomed to the gloom she started to scream hysterically; the bodies of her husband and father were turning slowly as they hung by their chins from hooks suspended in the ceiling. Pringle, on seeing her reaction, laughed evilly. Isobel Elliot ceased her tears and turned round and fixed the drunken old man with glittering eyes. *"May the memory of yer evil deeds haunt ye for ever, like the, hounds of hell may ye find no rest in this life or through eternity."* It all seems to have been too much for the servants; gradually they began to desert Buckholm Tower leaving George Pringle to a bitter, dissolute and solitary old age tormented, it is said, by the memories of the atrocities he had committed. He died in 1693 and was buried in Melrose Abbey. The inscription on his gravestone simply reads: *"Here Lyes George Pringle of Buckholme who deceased the 5 March, 1693, aged 78 years"*.

His son, who had little to do with his father for many years, became Laird of Buckholm. If local people thought that the *deil* had departed with the death of George Pringle, they were to be sadly disillusioned. Regularly at the midnight hour his spectre would appear in the tower. There would be a banging on the front door but when it was opened no one was there. Noises were heard coming from the dungeon, of such intensity that the whole tower vibrated. People swore that they could hear the sound of a man fleeing for his life and the baying of hounds. The local inhabitants were terrified; so much so that the local minister was called on to help rid them of the evil spirit.

The minister called upon was the Rev. Henry Davidson who was born at Eckford in 1687 and had been ordained minister at Galashiels in February 1714, a post he was to retain until his death forty-two years later. He was a man of quite independent views who in 1723, sixteen years after the Treaty of Union with England, called a fast day for, *"the late sinful union between England and Scotland."* His reaction to the petition by the residents in Buckholm has not been recorded but it must have set him quite a problem. On the one hand the Church was trying to rid the land of the superstitious beliefs that it considered part and parcel of recently overthrown Roman Catholicism. On the other hand, Henry Davidson had been born and brought up in the country and knew how powerful the belief in ghosts was among country people. His own personal beliefs are not known to us.

The minister resolved to act. As the anniversary of George Pringle's death approached, he gathered all the local people together with the household in the hall at Buckholm. As midnight approached he held a service and then made the congregation lock all the windows and doors. He then instructed them that under no circumstances should they leave the hall and that they should ask him no questions on his return. He left armed only with his bible, which he held firmly underneath his arm. The door was locked behind him. Long hours passed. The assembly waited fearfully; children whimpered in their mothers' arms, old men muttered in a fretful sleep and there was an air of tension that was long remembered. They could only imagine what kind of conversation was going on between the minister and the spirit of the dead laird. After what seemed like an eternity the minister returned. He entered the hall looking none the worse for his unearthly confrontation. He addressed the expectant congregation: *"Peace be with you all, let us return thanks to the Great Reliever of all our troubles, and henceforth know that the cause of your fears is laid to rest. Ask no questions, what has transpired can never be revealed."*

And it never has been revealed. But from that day no sight or sound of the *deil of Buckholm* has been reported.

Getting There

Buckholm Tower is on the outskirts of Galashiels. If you come down the A7 from Edinburgh you turn left about a mile from Galashiels on the road to Langshaw. About 50 yards on your right there is a track that takes you to Buckholm Tower. It is a walk of about half a mile and it would be good manners if the farmer is about to let him know where you are going. When you reach the tower it is immediately obvious what a strategic position it held. There are still hooks on the ceilings of the basement of the tower but not, I would suggest, of 17th century origin. However, it is better to be safe than sorry and I do not recommend a visit after dark.

Buckholm Tower

Merlin in The Borders

For almost a thousand years Merlin the Wizard, of the fabled court of King Arthur, has been linked with Tintagel in Cornwall, Glastonbury in Somerset and Snowdonia in Wales. Yet why is it that there is a persistent local tradition that Merlin was murdered on the banks of the river Tweed and buried there beside Drumelzier Church? To find the answer we have to examine how the story of Merlin became one of the enduring features of the literary landscape of Britain and draw aside part of the veil that covers much of the history of Dark Age Scotland.

Around 1136 Geoffrey of Monmouth, a monk of Welsh or Breton descent, wrote his *History of the Kings of Britain*. It was to become the first British best seller and had an immediate impact on the Anglo-Norman aristocracy who then ruled Britain and much of France. Geoffrey' History told a story that had never been heard before. For the first time the feudal aristocracy learned of the

The Haunted Borders

history of the Britons, who had been supplanted by the Angles and Saxons. It told of the exploits of King Arthur who fought against the Saxons and went on to conquer Europe. Merlin appears in it as the advisor of Arthur and as the man who prophesied the destruction of King Vortigern who had invited the Saxons into Britain and also as a master magician. So popular did this character of Merlin become, that Geoffrey followed up his success with *'The Prophecies of Merlin'*. The Normans of the time could identify with Geoffrey's version of British history for they were aware that the Bretons and the Welsh came from the same Celtic stock. The north-west area of France derived the name Britanny from those Britons who had fled across the channel from the Saxons. Many Bretons had come over with William the Conqueror in 1066; thus the Norman establishment was able to bask in the reflected glory of Geoffrey's heroic history of the British race. The Normans also took some pleasure in the fact that it showed the Anglo-Saxons in a very poor light. The stories of a lost Golden Age fitted in well with the troubled temper of Geoffrey's own times. Merlin's prophecies seemed to relate to events of current concern - not too surprising as Geoffrey had invented most of them! Such was the impact of the story on the popular imagination that when Henry II's heir was born in 1187, he was christened, *Arthur, the son of Geoffrey, Duke of Brittany, is born; the one hoped for by the people.*

In 1485 William Caxton published Thomas Malory's Mort d'Arthur in which the story of Merlin was developed along the lines with which we are familiar today. Once again the events of the times ensured its widespread popularity. A few weeks before its publication Richard III had been killed at the battle of Bosworth. The victor, Henry Tudor, was a prince with Welsh ancestry. One of Merlin's prophecies, that of the eventual triumph of the Welsh, seemed to many to have been fulfilled when Henry Tudor ascended the throne. The publication of Tennyson's *Merlin and Vivien* in 1859 firmly fixed Merlin in the popular imagination where he has remained ever since. Both Malory and Tennyson drew from Geoffrey's History and added to it. In the process they helped create a literary figure that has been further developed in fiction and in film. But how much of Geoffrey's History was drawn from historical fact and how much of it was the product of his imagination as well as of a desire to glorify his Welsh background?

There is evidence that Geoffrey drew much of his material from manuscripts that had preserved Welsh verses composed centuries before that and which had been copied down many times in the intervening period. Celtic narrative verse was essentially an oral medium; the early bards had a great distrust of the written word. Among a number of other functions, the Druids were not only priests but also soothsayers and bards who chronicled the history of their tribes and princes. With the arrival of the Romans, and more particularly of Christianity, the role of the Druids was undermined, but their function as storytellers and as repositories of the tribal lore was to continue among the bards. The bardic role was an important one in 6th century Britain. Every petty chief kept a bard who related the tribal history and sang the praises of the chief throughout the long and cold winter months. The skills of these bards were highly regarded and many of their tales were repeated and sung down over the centuries. One of the most celebrated of the 6th century bards was Aneirin who is credited with the authorship of the Gododdin, which tells the story of a British war band who marched off from Manau Gododdin to be defeated in a battle with the Angles. It is the product of a warlike and aristocratic society and has much in common with the Greek Homeric epics:

The men who went to Catraeth,
Wis the host; the grey mead their drink

As Greece had its Heroic Age with Homer as its bard, so did Welsh bards come to regard the second half of the 6th century as their 'Heroic Age.' The Gododdin was written in a form of ancient Welsh. It therefore came as a bit of a shock to Welsh scholars when they discovered that Manau Gododdin referred to part of the Lothians in Scotland and that the Gododdin capital was at Din Eidyn or what we now know as Edinburgh. Worse still, Aneirin was not born in what is now the Principality of Wales, but on the northern slopes of the Lammmermuir Hills. His epic poem relates the attempt to stop an Anglian advance on the Lothians and the battle took place at Catterick in North Yorkshire.

Aneirin, Taliesin and a number of other bards came to be called *Gwyr y Gogledd - Men of the North.* In the 6th century, despite pressure from Picts and Scots from the north and growing Anglian pressure from the south, a large swathe of the country, from the Humber to the Forth, was controlled by Celtic tribes united only by a common culture and a common language - Brythonic Welsh. The departure of the Romans had seen the re-emergence of many of the Celtic tribes who had never really fallen under the control of Rome. A number of kingdoms grew up; among them Rheged, which appears, at its peak to have stretched from the Humber to the Solway Firth with its major centre at Carlisle. There was Strathclyde, which encompassed most of Ayrshire and ranged from Loch Lomond to the river Tweed with its capital at Dun Alcuit or Dumbarton. The Gododdin were established in what are now the Lothians and Northumberland. It was a constantly changing and fluid situation. Despite threats from external enemies, the Britons were rarely able to unite under a single leader. Most of their energies were taken up with fighting among themselves.

A complicating factor was the revival of Christianity in the area. Christianity had originally been brought to these northern climes by Roman soldiers but had only really blossomed within the boundaries of the towns and major settlements; in the countryside the Celts tended to remain loyal to their old Celtic gods. Early Christian missionaries, such as Ninian and later Kentigern and Columba, had helped make most of the northern British tribes at least nominally Christian, but paganism had a habit of rearing its head every now and then. It was within this scenario, of pagan Celt warring against Christian Celt and at the same time trying to resist the encroachments of Pict, Scot, Angle and Saxon, that the name of Merlin first appears. One of the stories that emerges from the poetry of the bards of North Britain concerns Myrridyn. Geoffrey of Monmouth latinised the name as Merlinus. It is possible that Myrridyn was not so much a personal name as a title or professional name for a bard or counsellor to a king or tribal, chief. Whatever the case, the Welsh Annal tells a tale of Myrridyn bard and counsellor to Gwendollau, a pagan king who was killed at the battle of Arderydd in 573. Myrridyn went insane as a result of the savage slaughter that took place during the battle and wandered for many years in the Caledonian forest hunted by the men of Rhyderrich Hael, the victor at Arderydd. It is a story that is reflected in the *Life of St Kentigern.*

The battle of Arderydd is described in one of the Welsh triads as one of *The Three Futile battles of the Island of Britain.* Futile because it was another case of Briton fighting Briton instead of making common cause against the Angles and Saxons who were spreading remorselessly over the land. The battle was fought in 573 at a site near Longtown, just across the present border on the road to Carlisle. According to the Welsh Annals, the battle was fought over a *lark's nest*, almost certainly a reference to Caerlaverock in Dumfriesshire. Caerlaverock was to become an important medieval stronghold, but at this time it was a Celtic hill fort with a key strategic position to anyone wanting to expand westwards. While the battle could have been the result of the collision of the territorial ambitions of two Celtic chiefs, there is much evidence to suggest that it was also a climactic struggle between the forces of Paganism and Christianity.

Gwenddollau ab Ceido has a pedigree that is preserved in the Lineage of the Men of the North in Welsh manuscripts. He was sixth in descent from Coel Hen, whose territory included Galloway and Ayrshire and who was to become the Old King Cole of nursery rhyme fame. Gwenddollau's memory may be preserved in the name of the village Corwhinley near Longtown from Caer Wenddolau or Gwenddollau's fort. The evidence suggests that Gwenddollau was closely identified with the old Celtic pagan culture. In the Old Welsh *Triad of the Three Horses* the bard speaks of princes coming to see *The sacred fire of Gwenddollau in Arderydd* - a clear reference to the survival of pagan fire worship. Gwenddollau is also identified as one of the pagan *Bull Protectors of Britain*. It is not without significance that his adversary, Rhydderich Hael was to become known as the *Champion of Christendom*.

Rhydderich Hael is referred to by Adomman, the 7th century biographer of St Columba, *as son of Tudwal who reigned at Dumbarton*. After the battle of Arderydd, he emerges as the master of Strathclyde from Dumbarton down into present day Cumbria. Significantly, he recalled St Kentigern from Wales, the year after Arderydd. St Kentigern had fled there after an upsurge of paganism in Strathclyde. St Kentigern (or St Mungo) was to be closely identified with Rhydderich Hael and the establishment of the Celtic church in and around Glasgow. It would appear that after the battle of Arderydd, Christianity triumphed among the north Britons and paganism was driven underground. It also established Rhydderich Hael as ruler of all the North British kingdoms. Arderydd was, without doubt, one of the significant battles in Dark Age Britain.

The Welsh Annals state that the battle was fought in the *field between Liddel and Carwonlow*. Just to the north of Longtown there is a stream called the Carwinelow that flows into the Esk where that river merges with the Liddel. Above this river junction rise the huge earthen ramparts of what was once a medieval castle and before this it was a Celtic hill fort. Local tradition has it that the battle reached a climax in the field below these ramparts. Arderydd itself, the court of Gwenddollau, was situated on the top of the highest of the two hills that make up Arthuret Knowes about two miles to the south of Longtown. The battle was long remembered for its ferocity and, unusually, lasted for several days after Gwenddollau fell.

His men fought on until they were all slaughtered within the ramparts of the fort. This dreadful slaughter together with the death of his patron and the victory of a religion he abhorred, caused Merlin, bard and advisor, and possibly Gwenddollau's battle strategist, to lose his reason.

At this point two different narrative traditions begin to merge. There is the Welsh Merlin/Myrridyn poetry, fragments of which are ascribed to Merlin himself, and the Strathclyde St Kentigern stories. Both agree that Merlin became mad after the death of his patron and fled into depths of the Caledonian forest that covered most of southern Scotland. It was within this vast area that Merlin wandered, overcome by grief at the carnage that had been Arderydd, at the death of Gwenddollau and the loss of all that he held dear:

Now I sleep not, I tremble for my lord
My sovereign Gwenddollau, and my fellow countrymen
After enduring wickedness and grief in the Forest of Celyddon.

Merlin had obviously been an important figure at Gwenddollau's court:

And in the battle of Arderydd my torque was of gold

It is quite possible that he was of royal blood and that this was one of the reasons why Rhydderich Hael was so keen to capture him. He sends his soldiers out to capture Merlin who evades them by hiding in the branches of an apple tree

Sweet apple tree which grows in a glade
Its peculiar power hides me from the men of Rhydderich.

The apple tree had a special significance for the pagan Celt. St Kentigern was, in many ways, the Christian counterpart of the pagan Merlin. He was the advisor to Rhydderich Hael and was himself a Celt who would have been well acquainted with pagan customs. His biography was written by some of his followers shortly after his death and they would have wanted to display him in a very positive light. They would have used his life story as a weapon against the old pagan religions that still survived among country folk. In the St Kentigern story, the saint is supposed to have met a hairy, naked madman in the forest who told him that he had been driven mad in a terrible battle. St Kentigern took pity on him and converted the poor wretch to Christianity. That Merlin would have been seen as a threat to the new Christian order is very likely and the monk-historians would have been keen to establish St Kentigern's superiority.

Madman or mystic, Merlin roamed the length and breadth of the Caledonian Forest; a man who had lost everything he held dear -his lord, his religion and his country. He grew old in the woods of Caledon, subsisting on roots and berries and living like an animal of the forest. It was said that he foretold his own death, which he declared would happen in three ways; by beating, by drowning and by stabbing. He was, according to the St Kentigern/Strathclyde stories, killed by some shepherds of a local chieftain named Meldedus. First, he was beaten and then flung into the river Tweed where he was impaled on an underwater salmon stake. According to the tale it happened on a steep bank of the Tweed at Dunmeller - or Drumelzier. The site of his death has long been held to be the point where the Powsail burn flows into the Tweed. In 603 Aidan MacGabrain, king of Dalriada, who was accused by Merlin of having betrayed Gwenddollau at Arderydd, tried to stem the remorseless Anglian tide of invasion at Dawston in Liddesdale. He failed and was probably killed in the battle. As a result of this defeat Lothian and Galloway fell under Anglian control. Later in another victory, this time at the battle of Chester, the Anglians drove a wedge between the Britons of Wales and their kinsmen of Cumbria and Strathclyde. The heroic age of *The Men of the North* was over. The bards slowly departed from the North taking with them their poetry and their stories to the more fertile literary fields of Wales. Among those stories was that of *the wild man of the forest*, which was to be resurrected by Geoffrey of Monmouth as the legend of Merlin.

In the North, Strathclyde was to remain an independent British kingdom almost up to the arrival of the Normans. Thereafter their language and culture began to disappear leaving only vague and fragmentary echoes. But the story of Merlin, or Myrridyn, or Lailoken, who was the spiritual champion of old Celtic paganism, is undoubtedly a story of Strathclyde and the Borders. Merlin would never have been able to identify himself with the nation that was to become Scotland; but his cry, which still echoes down the centuries, is the cry of a man who has lost his sense of identity and for whom all life has lost its meaning; the man whose despair has been preserved in the pages of The Black Book of Carmarthen-

> *Since the battle of Arderydd I care not*
> *Were the sky to fall and the sea to overflow.*

Getting There

From Peebles take the A72 towards Carnwath. Turn left up the B712, after about 5 miles you will come to the village of Drumelzier. The church is on the right hand side of the road. If you walk down the path to the church following the course of the Powsail burn you will come to the spot where the burn joins the river Tweed. Here is the traditional place where the great Merlin was said to have been killed and buried.

Where Powsail meets Tweed

Neidpath Tower

The Maid of Neidpath

Oh, lovers' eyes are sharp to see,
And lovers' ears in hearing;
And love, in life's extremity,
Can lend an hour of cheering!
Disease had been in Mary's bower
And slow decay from mourning;
Though now she sits on Neidpath's tower
To watch her Love's returning.

All sunk and dim her eyes so bright,
Her form decay'd by pining,
Till through her wasted hand, at night,
You saw the taper shining.
By fits a sultry hectic hue
Across her cheek was flying;
By fits so ashy pale she grew
Her maidens thought her dying.

These are the first two stanzas from Sir Walter Scott's celebrated and romantic poem. He wrote it a short while after staying at Neidpath castle in Peebles where he absorbed many of the tales and traditions of the castle and the surrounding countryside.

Neidpath castle stands on high rock overhanging a sudden bend in the river Tweed. It has dominated the surrounding landscape for centuries and it impresses through its strength, rather than architectural elegance. It is built on the site of an ancient Cymric settlement, the word Nedd denotes a stream that forms whirls or turns, in the Welsh that was once spoken here. In time the Cymri were displaced by Saxon incomers and their word, poeth, meaning a steep and narrow way, was added and, over time, the name emerged as the familiar Neidpath. The building dates from the 14th century, but was substantially remodelled in the 16th century. Upper stories were added, and again in the 17th century.

From the 12th century, the dominant family in the area was the Fraziers, whose surname developed into Fraser. They were among the first wave of Norman incomers into Scotland and became Lords of Tweeddale with Neidpath as their main stronghold. The most famous of this family was Sir Simon Fraser who is said to have defeated the English three times in one day during the wars of Independence. He was later captured and put to death. Neidpath passed into the hands of the Hay family, one of whom had married Sir Simon Fraser's daughter. It was the Hays who built the current tower and they were to own it until it was sold to Douglas, Duke of Queensberry in 1686. He bought it for his son, William Douglas, Earl of March.

It is an odd experience reading through the lineages of aristocratic families. It was, of course, very important to them, that the bloodlines be carefully recorded in order to maintain ownership of property. So when we delve into a page of the family tree of the Douglas family, we find that William Douglas, 2nd Earl of March married Anne Douglas-Hamilton, Countess of Ruglen . William was born in 1696 and died at the early age of 34 in 1730. He had six children who, strangely for their time and class all died unmarried. The eldest son, who was to become the 4th Duke of Queensberry and Earl of Ruglen went on to lead a dissolute life. He died in 1810. He had two brothers and three sisters who all died before him unmarried. They thus become mere footnotes in the family tree unremembered and almost forgotten. One of his sisters, probably the youngest, was Jean Douglas, though her date of birth or death is not recorded. Poor Jean is merely noted in the records as having died unmarried. Yet around this young woman there has sprung up one of the most romantic of stories that is associated with Neidpath Castle.

Jean Douglas met young Walter Scott of Tushielaw, possibly at a social gathering. They found that they were strongly attracted to each other. They had to meet secretly for both were aware that her father would never countenance her marrying someone so far beneath her in social status. For although the Scotts of Tushielaw were of an ancient family, they were still regarded as small lairds. Eventually word got out, as it always does, and William Douglas was furious. He ordered that the young couple never see each other again and to make sure, it was arranged that Walter would be sent abroad. But instead of gradually forgetting him, Jean pined for her lost love and became ill. The family became alarmed at the deterioration in Jean as she lost weight and became listless.

She had contracted consumption, a not uncommon affliction in young women of the time. Finally, it was decided to summon

Walter back from abroad. Young Walter immediately organised his return and as soon as he landed mounted his horse and rode to Peebles. Meanwhile, Jean had rallied and moved into her father's townhouse that was on the main road. She sat in the balcony, still pale and wan, but excited at the prospect of seeing her lover again. Soon the lone rider was spied. Jean stood up to wave to him. He glanced up but galloped on, desperate to get to Neidpath where he thought that Jean awaited him. He had not recognized the girl on the balcony as his Jean so frail and emaciated had she become. When he galloped past, Jean had a seizure from which she never recovered. Some were to say that she died from a broken heart.

The ghost of Jean Douglas is said to haunt Neidpath castle. She is described as wearing a brown dress with a large white collar and as having long black hair. It is said that she does not like to hear people laughing or being seen to enjoy themselves and shows her displeasure by banging doors. She passes through solid walls and has been seen both inside the castle and also in the courtyard and at some of the surrounding walks. It is almost as if her restless spirit cannot bring itself to depart from the place where she experienced such happiness, however brief.

Getting There

From the High Street in Peebles head west and turn right on to the A72. After about three quarters of a mile take a left into Neidpath Castle.

Pearlin Jean

That ghosts, fairies and other supernatural beings existed, was accepted unquestioningly by our Scottish ancestors. Wide-eyed children would be entertained by a grandmother who could identify a nearby ruin or wood that had been the scene of a supernatural encounter. In time these children would entertain their own offspring with the tales of ghosts, ghoulies and strange happenings in their local area. If the details were changed a bit to improve the dramatic effect so much the better. This was more likely to happen as the events on which the story was originally based receded further back in time. But times change; families moved from the country to the town, others sailed across the seas and most of us have travelled far from the homes of our ancestors. People were busier, new forms of entertainment were developed and children had less time and perhaps less inclination to listen to their old granny's stories. She would, in any case, refer to places they had no knowledge of and to a way of life that was quite

The Haunted Borders

alien to them. The growth of education was perhaps the most significant factor in the decline of belief in ghosts. The advance of science and technology with its emphasis on the logical and rational permeated all levels of society and gradually belief in the old ghosts began to disappear.

Yet a story of a supernatural event that persisted in a locality often had more than just a good story to it. Something so unusual had happened that it lingered in the minds of people long after those involved had died and details of the actual events became vague. So it is with the story of 'Pearlin Jean', at one time probably the most famous apparition in Scotland and around whom a number of versions of her tale have grown. As is the case in most stories with supernatural associations the documentary evidence is scant but the tradition was such a powerful one in Berwickshire that the story is well known even today.

The ancient mansion of the Allanbank estate stood on the north bank of the river Blackadder up until the middle of the 19th century. It had been in the hands of the Stuart family for many years. Towards the end of the 17th century the owner was Robert Stuart, born in 1643, who in 1687 was made a Baronet, but was just plain Mr. Stuart up until then. The Stuarts of Allanbank were of an ancient lineage, being descended from a younger brother of the founder of the Royal House of Stuart. However, the then current incumbent was one who devoted much of his time to wine, women and the card table, to the consternation and scandal of his neighbours.

Robert was said to be very handsome and could be charming when it was required. He travelled frequently on the continent, as many young wealthy men did at that time, and it was on one of these trips that he met a beautiful but impressionable young girl called Jeanne. Some accounts say she was Italian, others that she was French, but most tell us that she was the daughter of a Flemish Jew. Perhaps the fact that the only versions of the story that have come down to us are from the oral memory of the locals accounts for the discrepancies in the stories of her origins. What is certain is that Robert returned with a beautiful young foreign girl who could not speak English and who took great delight in wearing fine silk lace. The Scots word for such lace was 'pearlin' and thus the girl became known as Pearlin Jean.

Despite the fact that the couple were not made welcome by the Berwickshire gentry they were quite content in each other's company. The servants and local tenants took to the master's pretty young lass for she had a lively and kind manner that charmed all who came in contact with her. But as is often the way of such affairs, Robert gradually grew tired of his new, young love. She became pregnant and bore him a daughter but he began to spend more of his time away from home. Eventually he would stay in Edinburgh for several months leaving Jeanne and her child to fend for themselves. All the while the servants watched and sympathised but were unable to do much to help the unhappy girl.

One day a messenger arrived with a letter from Robert saying that he was returning with a bride and that he wanted the girl and her child to remove themselves from his house. If she did this with no fuss or scandal he would settle a small allowance on her. The next day the heartbroken Jeanne and her child left Allanbank and could not be found anywhere. Robert had married, not for love, but for money. His new wife was the daughter of Sir John Gilmour, head of an old Edinburgh family. As the newly weds were driven up the avenue to the house, Jeanne suddenly started out of the bushes and flung herself in front of the carriage, her baby daughter still in her arms. The baby survived but Jeanne was killed instantly.

One version of the tale tells us that Robert was so overcome by remorse that he decided, in spite of his new wife's objections, to bring up Jeanne's daughter as his own. Whether he did so is not clear and I would certainly prefer to believe that the daughter would have been sent back to Jeanne's heartbroken parents. To his new wife's chagrin Robert commissioned a portrait of Jeanne that hung in the bedroom of the house for many years. It would have been a constant reminder to him of his dreadful behaviour and whether it was the prompting of a guilty conscience or something altogether more unearthly he was heard to plead for forgiveness from Jeanne almost as if she were in the room beside him. Soon servants and visitors began to see Jeanne's ghost, dressed in her pearlin or lace gliding through the house. Others heard her familiar laughter or the rustle of her dress. Robert grew more morose and showed all the signs of sinking into what we would now call a deep depression. His marriage withered. Despite the fact that his wife bore him two children, she could not compete with the presence of Pearlin Jean. She left with the children leaving Robert with his ghostly lover.

Robert was knighted in 1687 and apparently carrying on a successful career as a merchant in Edinburgh. He died in 1707. But the ghost of Jeanne continued to haunt the old house and its grounds. The bedroom where her portrait hung was left untouched, the ashes of a fire, lit half a century before were left where they lay. The estate passed through another four generations of Stewarts and was sold when the last Baronet died in 1849. In the meantime Allanbank had acquired an unenviable reputation throughout Berwickshire. Visitors to the house heard the sounds of doors opening and closing and conversation would suddenly cease as the rustle of a silken dress was heard in an empty hallway. Seven ministers were called in to try to lay Jeanne's unquiet spirit. Eventually the servants grew used to Jeanne's presence, to them she became as familiar a part of the old mansion as the furniture and the drapes. She would appear to have retained the same mischievous sense of humour that she had possessed in life. Thomas Blackadder was a young labourer on the Alanbank estate. He was courting, Jenny, one of the maidservants from the 'big hoose' and had arranged to meet her in the orchard at dusk. As he was waiting he saw a figure dressed in white come running towards him through the trees. Laughing he ran towards her but she disappeared. He stopped and turned to see her at the far end of the orchard. He ran towards her again only for her to disappear leaving a trail of light laughter in the autumn air. A few moments later Jenny arrived, still dressed in her dark working clothes. She had been relieved from her domestic duties only seconds before and had seen nothing out of the ordinary in the orchard. Long years later when she was an old lady, Jenny still remembered how much she had been affected by Thomas Blackadder's terror.

The new owners of Allanbank estate decided that they would demolish the old house and build a new one on the bank above Blackadder. At the time, the demolition of the original house caused great consternation in the neighbourhood. *Where will*

Pearlin Jean gang noo? they asked. Some claim that her restless spirit can still be seen especially at the gloaming of an autumn evening. Others felt that with the demise of the ill-fated mansion of the Stuarts that Jeanne's spirit had at last found the peace that had escaped her in her mortal life.

Getting There

Allanbank House was situated about 4 miles outside Duns. You take the A6105 Duns to Chirnside road and turn right up the B6437 road to Allanton. Just over a mile down the road on the right there is a private house and studios called Allanbank Courtyard. This building has been converted out of the old stable building of the original estate. Just past this there is a track. A little way along this there is a field on the left, which is probably the site of the original Allanbank House. There was no indication of Pearlin Jean's presence when I was there but I was assured that the general atmosphere of peace and benevolence is partly due to her continued presence.

The Mystery of the Foul Ford

It stands about fifty yards off the Westruther road just beside the track that wends its way across the desolate moorlands that stretch beyond the Berwickshire town of Greenlaw. It is a rough-hewn, upright stone in a small hollow with no inscription to explain why it is there. It is not an ancient stone but was obviously placed with some purpose in mind. I had long been intrigued when I first came across it, but it was to take many years before I managed to discover the strange and eerie tale behind the stone's presence on the bleak foothills of the Lammermuirs.

Greenlaw Moor has always been a wild and barren place. It stretches along the lower slopes of the Lammermuir Hills that divide Berwickshire from the Lothians. Not many travellers set foot in it nowadays but at one time, when people were more used to walking long distances, it was crossed by travellers making their way from Kelso and Greenlaw through the Lammermuir villages and then into Lothian. It had to be travelled with care. The mist could descend with great swiftness and it was not unknown for unwary travellers to find themselves wandering through the moor, far from the paths and despairing of ever finding their way back. Some never came out alive. Winter or late autumn were the danger times for the unwary.

In the heart of the Lammermuir hills lies the village of Longformacus. It is situated on the Dye Water within a few miles of its junction with the Whitadder, a tributary of the river Tweed. Longformacus is still a sleepy village, picturesque and isolated, surrounded by hills and moorland. At the beginning of the nineteenth century, it was even more isolated, before our road systems were improved. Belief in the supernatural hung around here long after the hill folk's more sophisticated neighbours in the Merse to the south and Haddington in the north, had abandoned it. It was, in many ways, a small closed world where life went on as it always had where little ever changed.

By the end of the eighteenth century the Niel family had been established as blacksmiths for many generations in the village of Longformacus. Tradition has it that the family name was originally MacNiel and that an ancestor had been out with the Jacobite army of 1715 in which he had been a farrier. Another story is that this ancestor had fled from the Highlands to escape local justice. He could have been one of the troop of Highlanders who passed through Longformacus during the 1715 Jacobite rebellion. On spotting the piles of newly-cut wood laid aside for the rebuilding of Longformacus House they decided to make a fire of it to keep themselves warm during the night. Whatever his reasons, the Highland-born MacNiel decided that this sleepy

Borders village was a more congenial place to stay than his native glen. He settled there and in time his son, Robert, became the blacksmith in Longformacus.

They were a wild lot these Niels. Robert Niel was brought up before the Kirk Session where he had to promise to abstain from all *cursing and swearing*. In 1736 he and his wife, Agnes Auld, were rebuked by the session for their irregular marriage and had to promise to *live as married persons and Christians*. In 1779 Robert's son, John, was in trouble when he was accused of uncleanliness with Isobel Chirnside. John at first denied this but later he was to confess that he was the father of her child. The following year he married Janet Lunham. Such public shaming did not deter John Niel, however, for a few years later he was again in front of the Kirk Session. This time he and his brother, Francis, were accused of fighting with John Dun. It was not so much the brawling that the Session was concerned about but the fact that it took place on the Sabbath. Francis was to die young shortly afterwards but John's date with destiny was to be a strange and mysterious one and the repercussions were to affect the next generation of his family - and perhaps beyond.

John Niel had the reputation of being rather aggressive when he had been drinking. His family were thus a bit fearful when he set out to attend his sister's funeral in the nearby town of Greenlaw in January of 1805. At that time Scottish funerals featured a great deal of drinking and there is no reason to believe that this one was any different and that John Niel would not imbibe freely. Burials and funerals were fraught with dangers for the superstitious Celt. There were all kinds of rituals to be gone through in order to protect oneself from being harmed by the jealous spirits of the recent dead. John Niel, with his Highland background, would have been thoroughly familiar with the world of the supernatural. It would have seemed as real to him as the hills, trees and rivers that made up part of his natural world. Did the winter January sun shine on John Niel's face during the funeral? This was a sure sign that he would be the next to die. Maybe he stumbled as he helped carry his sister's corpse to the graveyard. If he did, this would also mark him out as being the next to leave this life. Whatever the reasons we know that John Niel was thoroughly depressed when he left Greenlaw in mid-afternoon, after the funeral, to walk the long road home to Longformacus; a road that took him across Greenlaw Moor.

On his way he met Robert Wilson, the shepherd at Blacksmill, who was afterwards to remark that John Niel seemed pale and dejected as he made his way along the south side of Dirrington Law and approached a place known as the Foul Ford, about halfway between Greenlaw and Longformacus. By this time dusk was falling. At home his family waited expectantly. Night fell and as midnight approached there was still no sign of John Niel. Suddenly the worried family heard a crash outside their door. When they opened it they found John Niel lying unconscious on the ground. He was carried indoors and put to bed where he lay delirious and raving for the rest of the night and most of the following day. By that evening he had recovered sufficiently to ask that the minister, the Reverend Selby Ord, come to see him. When the minister arrived, John insisted on speaking to him alone. After the minister had left he called his family together. He made them promise, one by one, that they would never cross the moor at the Foul Ford after the sun had set. The family were by this time quite terrified for it was obvious to them that John Niel was a dying man and they readily agreed to his demands. The next morning John Niel died. There was no obvious cause of death as he had always been a robust and healthy person.

The circumstances surrounding the death of John Niel caused a great sensation in the village of Longformacus. But gradually the memory of it began to fade and life went on as it always had in the hill village. John's son, Henry, took over his father's blacksmith's business. Henry Niel was a tall, strong man who had a reputation for being a good workman. One autumn day he went to Floors Castle to settle some accounts with the Duke of Roxburgh's factor. On his way back, he stopped off in Greenlaw to visit an old friend, James Richardson, who was a gravedigger as well as being a parish officer and the pair of them retired to a local hostelry. Later, Henry had some tea at James Richardson's house after which he prepared to make the long walk home to Longformacus. James said he would walk part of the way with him. The most obvious and shortest way to get from Greenlaw to Longformacus is to strike up the Moss road from the Duns road and across the moor. James was surprised when his companion passed the Moss road turn-off and asked him why he was taking such a long route to get home. Henry then told him about the promise he had made his father not to travel by the Foul Ford after the sun had set. James Richardson laughed at his friend's superstitions and told him that, in any case, he had lots of time to get past the Foul Ford before it got dark. Henry, possibly a bit embarrassed at appearing so superstitious, put his fears behind him, waved good-bye to his friend and set off along the Moss road towards the Foul Ford.

Silently a fog started to rise and slowly spread over the moor. No doubt as he peered through the enveloping mist, Henry recalled to himself the circumstances of his father's death and feelings of nameless dread started to creep over him. However, he was a sensible man and tried to brush aside the gnawing fears and quickened his pace in order to make sure he got through the Foul Ford before the darkening. He was delighted when he caught up with John Michie, the blacksmith from Spottiswoode, who was also making his way home. John Michie noticed that Henry was quite agitated and tried to persuade him to take the longer road around the moor which would have avoided the Foul Ford, for he was familiar with the story of Henry's father and anyway, was a bit nervous of the Foul Ford himself. Henry replied that he wanted to get home quickly and tried to get the other man to accompany him. John Michie demurred. Henry Niel left and was quickly swallowed up by the ever-thickening mist.

The next morning Adam Redpath, a drain digger, was passing the Ford. As he approached it, he saw something lying on the ground. It was the lifeless body of Henry Niel. There appeared to have been no signs of violence on his body but his face was twisted with an expression that seemed to suggest he had died in great agony and terror. Adam Redpath also noticed that most of Henry's clothes were strewn along the track behind him. He was also to remark on the curious fact that those clothes that Henry was wearing were on back to front. It appeared to those who came to gaze on the scene that Henry Niel had been fleeing from some unknown terror.

Henry Niel's death caused a sensation in the village and in the surrounding area. By this time the Reverend Selby Ord was dead, but he had told his housekeeper, Mrs Deans, about the story that John Niel had related to him so many years before. She felt that the death of Henry Niel now freed her from the promise that she had made to the minister not to tell anyone about it. And it was a strange tale she had to tell.

According to John Niel, as he approached the Foul Ford on his way home from his sister's funeral, he saw a long cavalcade of riders coming two by two along the track. As they came closer in the gathering gloom he recognized among the riders, friends and relatives who were all long dead. Among them was his sister whom he had helped bury that morning. At the back of the column was a masked man with a feather in his hat who, while riding one horse, led another with an empty saddle. John Niel was urged to mount the spare horse. The blacksmith was transfixed with terror. He tried to flee but was seized. He continued to refuse to mount the horse offered to him and was eventually released only after he had given an undertaking that the first member of his family to cross the Foul Ford after dark would have to take his place. John Niel had tried to thwart this when he made his family promise not to cross the moor at night.

A few years later the stone was erected by John Scott of Spottiswoode to mark the spot where Henry Niel's body had been found. The Foul Ford after dark became a place to be avoided by the local population for many years. Today the land has been drained and the ford has gone but there is still a bleakness in the landscape though it retains little of the eerie atmosphere that it possessed when John and Henry Niel made their fateful journeys.

It was only when I came across a book on Highland folklore that the full significance of Henry being found with some of his clothes on back to front became apparent to me. It was a belief of the Highlander that if you were being chased by the ghosts of the dead turning your clothes around would confuse them and make them head off in the opposite direction. Henry Niel would still have been enough of a Highlander to subscribe to that belief.

The Niel family did not tarry long in Longformacus. Robert Niel, a nephew of Henry's became an innkeeper in Longformacus for a while before he emigrated to the United States with his family. I would imagine that his descendants would be in no hurry to visit the ancestral home in the Lammermuirs.

Getting There

The Foul Ford lies about 4 miles to the south west of Duns. You take A6105 road from Duns to Greenlaw and then turn right up the B6456 to Westruther. On your right-hand side as you turn off is the ancient farm of Choicelea which dates from the 14th century. About mile up the road you should be able to spot the monument on the left about a hundred yards from the road. A little way on, there is a gate and a red rock track leading down to the monument. The Foul Ford is very different from what it would have been like in John Niel's day. Then it would have been an evil-smelling bog that people would have avoided after dark even if they did not believe it was haunted. Today the Foul Ford has been drained but it still retains a desolate and lonely appearance. You can still walk the route the Niels, father and son, took on their fateful journeys

The Haunted Borders

and a pleasant walk it is on a summer's day. A word of advice - if you do intend to walk there leave early and make sure you are past the Foul Ford by sunset!

The Foul Ford

The Haunted Borders

The Auld Brig, Jedburgh

The Witches of Jedburgh

Jedburgh only emerges into the light of recorded history in the 11th century when its castle was firmly established as a favourite place of Scottish kings. Many royal charters were issued from there and Malcolm IV died within its walls in 1165. Jedburgh was even then, however, an ancient place. A church stood for three centuries before the magnificent abbey was built on its site at the beginning of the 12th century. Before this it had been an important centre for the Welsh speaking British tribes. The most important in the Jedburgh area were the Selgovae, a warlike people in whose territory the Romans felt it necessary to establish camps and send out frequent patrols. It was the Anglo-Saxons, however, who gave the place its name - Gedwearde - *the settlement on the river Jed.* Its situation on a fertile site close by the Jed and its position on that important Roman thoroughfare that is Dere Street were to make it one of the busiest early settlements in the Scottish Borders.

The building of the abbey and its elevation into a royal burgh made Jedburgh one of the most important and wealthy places in southern Scotland. This was also to have its disadvantages. It made the town an attractive target for English invaders throughout the four centuries of intermittent Anglo-Scottish warfare. Although it was not enclosed within fortified walls, like most medieval towns, Jedburgh was well defended by six strong towers and a powerful castle. The constant threat of invasion helped to create a frontier mentality among the townsfolk who proved to be tough-minded and resourceful at defending themselves, as indeed they had to be if they were to survive as a community. For most of the 14th century, however, the English occupied the castle. In 1409, when it was recaptured, the castle was dismantled stone by stone rather than allow it to fall into the hands of the English again. Despite the loss of the castle, Jedburgh continued to exist as an important strategic centre. It was attacked and destroyed many times but was always rebuilt. However, in the years 1544/45 the town was subjected to particularly ferocious English assaults, with the result that the abbey was reduced to ruins and its monks left, never to return. Like the rest of the Borders, 16th century Jedburgh was a place impoverished by war and inured to violence and civil unrest. War brings with it famine, disease and the breakdown of social order. These conditions together with the rise of zealous clergy helped to create a poisonous climate in Scotland in which many women were persecuted as witches. Jedburgh was a town that was to become infamous for its witches.

The records of witchcraft trials are very sparse; their absence, however, does not mean that they did not take place. Jedburgh is mentioned quite often in old records as a place where many people were accused of witchcraft. Indeed, if we were to assume that all those who were accused of witchcraft in Jedburgh actually came from the town, then Jedburgh would certainly qualify as a place where persecution was at its most intense. It was, however, a royal burgh and seat of the King's justice and it is likely that many of those accused came from outside the burgh. But the records are scarce, most of them have been destroyed, and it is likely that there were considerably more witchcraft trials than are currently recorded. Consider, for example, the excuse that the Provost of Jedburgh gave to the General Assembly in Edinburgh saying he could not attend, ...*next Wednesday on account of the burning of the witches*. There are no accounts of the trials of these witches so we do not know if this was an exceptional case or just one of many that the Burgh Provost had to attend. Where we find that people have been accused of witchcraft it is only occasionally that we discover whether they were acquitted, executed, or as sometimes happened, died in custody. In May 1671 no fewer than seven persons, six females and one male were accused of witchcraft and were lingering in Jedburgh jail. We know nothing of their ultimate fate.

It was dangerous to be poor, elderly and female in Jedburgh in the

The Haunted Borders

17th century. Meg Spinnie was an old woman who lived close to the Square. Tom Henderson, a local butcher, saw a cat running away with a piece of meat in its mouth. Enraged, he flung a stone at it that struck the cat on the leg. The next day old Meg Spinnie was found in her bed nursing an injured leg. There was no doubt in the minds of the Jedburgh folk that Meg was a witch who could turn herself into a cat. A similar incident concerned another old Jedburgh woman, called Nell Pinkerton, who lived in the Townhead. One day a hare had run up the lane, where she lived, chased by a pack of dogs. The next morning Nell was laid up in bed with sores on her heels that were immediately assumed to be dog bites. It was said that she was dragged from her bed, quickly condemned and burned. There was no such thing as coincidence in the lives of our forebears. They believed in cause and effect but not in any scientific way. Take for instance the case of Learmond, a Jedburgh cobbler. An old woman came into his shop and asked for a pair of shoes on credit. When he refused she turned away muttering under her breath. Next day Learmond's house in the Canongate burned down. Straight away he recalled the old woman's muttered threats and put the blame on her for his misfortune.

Among the annals of the Jedburgh witches perhaps the most celebrated case was that of Brown the local schoolmaster. It was claimed that he was a man of great piety and a pillar of the community. His wife though was something else. She did not attend church and was seen to roundly abuse her husband at every opportunity. Along with a number of neighbouring wives they made the life of the poor schoolmaster an absolute misery. The elders of the kirk were later to relate how his wife and some of her cronies had tied the hapless man up and dragged him across the stones of the river Jed. He constantly claimed that his wife was a witch and that she was in league with the devil. It would appear, however, that the local community took little note of his complaints until one morning when his lifeless body was found in a deep pool of the Jed. Peoples' memories were suddenly revived. On the night of his death the elders of the kirk had accompanied the schoolmaster back to his home but had fled when his wife had turned a torrent of abuse on them. Some people in the Canongate claimed they had been woken up by the schoolmaster loudly singing the 23rd Psalm as he was dragged down to the river by his wife and her fellow witches; they did not actually say if they had peeked out of their windows at the bizarre procession. It was also stated, on very good authority that on that same night fairies had been seen dancing on the top of Jedburgh Abbey. For our credulous ancestors this was proof enough. Perhaps the seven people accused of witchcraft in 1671 were the schoolmaster's wife and her neighbours. An alternative explanation, of what happened, is that the schoolmaster was quite insane and that he committed suicide. But this is a 21st century explanation and our ancestors would not have recognized many forms of mental illness.

Sometimes the person accused of witchcraft did fight back. In 1662 Patrick Johnstoun, described as a cordwainer in Jedburgh, appealed to the Privy Council that his wife was imprisoned in the Tolbooth in Jedburgh on a charge of witchcraft. He wanted a speedy trial so that if she was innocent she could be freed and returned home. In this case it is obvious that the husband thought that his wife was an innocent victim of the scandalmongering that was to condemn many women. It also took a certain amount of courage on his part to be seen defending an accused witch as this could bring down suspicion on himself. Let us hope that Patrick Johnstoun was successful in his efforts for the records are silent.

The normal method of execution for those found guilty of witchcraft was to be burned at the stake. If the authorities were feeling merciful, then the victims were strangled before being consigned to the flames. Executions were public spectacles designed to instil in those watching a sense of the awful power of those in authority. Hence the reason why it was more important for the Provost of Jedburgh to attend the *burning of the witches* rather than the General Assembly of the church. It is thought that the last witch to be burned in Jedburgh was Margaret Shortreed in 1696. Tradition has it that she was burned at a spot called Wildcatgait just outside Jedburgh on the Oxnam road. Wildcatgait is on the lee side of Doom Hill, which was probably an ancient place of execution for criminals and witches. It is likely that here was situated the Beggars Muir where other witches were supposed to have been burnt. In the early years of the nineteenth century a piece of stone with a square hole in the middle was found in this place which long afterwards retained an air of darkness for Jedburgh folk

Although the laws against witchcraft were repealed in the early 18th century the old beliefs did not give way easily. In 1775 it is recorded that a woman in Ancrum was 'scored' on her forehead. This was supposed to be an effective method of protecting oneself against witches. It is much easier to change the law than to change long held beliefs and prejudices.

Getting There

Jedburgh is now divided by the A68. The Canongate where the hapless Mr Brown was led down to the Jed by his wife and her cronies leads from he Market Square down to the A68. The Canongate at one time was the main entry into Jedburgh via the old bridge over the Jed that Charles Edward Stuart crossed with the Jacobite army in 1745. If you take the left turn up the Oxnam road about a mile and a half on the left-hand side is the place called Wildcatgait. At one time it was part of the Hartrigge estate and led into the Beggars Muir where Jedburgh burnt its witches. The hill leading up to this place was formerly known as Doom Hill. In an age conscious of property values, this has been changed to the more comfortable sounding –Dounehill

Hermitage Castle

Nightmare Castle

We do not know exactly when Hermitage castle was built. The stream beside the present castle was originally known as the Marching Burn, but at the end of the 12th century the site was inhabited by a reclusive hermit and it was from this individual that the castle, and the water beside it was to derive its name. Around the same time the land was held by a Norman family by the name of De Bolebeck. They may have been responsible for some of the earthworks whose remains can still be seen beside the present castle. It is likely that the first castle was built on the motte of an earlier structure. Being surrounded by bog and marsh would have made it easily defensible. It would have been needed, for the Norman incomers would have faced a native population bitterly resentful of these ruthless, alien intruders.

The De Soulis family appear as Lords of Liddesdale in the reign of David I. They were already a powerful family, possessing lands in Northamptonshire and in Haddington where their name is preserved in the village of Saltoun or Soulistoun. It is with this family that Hermitage was to develop its sinister reputation. In 1207, monastic records tell us that a Ranulph de Soulis was *assassinated by his domestics.* This Ranulph was the nephew of the first Lord of Liddesdale. It could be that this incident reflected the hostility that then existed between the native serfs and their Norman masters, or were the De Soulis family particularly harsh in their treatment of the Scottish peasantry? It is probable that the murder of Ranulph took place at the site of the old castle on the Liddell Crags around which the original village of Castletown grew.

The village that huddled beside the castle, on the junction of the Hermitage and Liddell rivers, would have been a miserable collection of hovels. The inhabitants had to labour on their lord's land and he could summon them for military service whenever he required. He had the right of *pit and gallows*, which allowed him to hang men and drown women as he deemed fit. Though nominally Christian, native culture had powerful pagan undertones; the old Norse and Celtic gods were still invoked. A belief in magic, witchcraft and sorcery underpinned the lives of the common folk. On a ridge two miles north of the village stood a stone circle - a sacred place to their pagan forebears. It is known as Nine Stane Rig and it was to play an important part in the folk memories of the De Soulis family.

In 1244 Henry III announced that *a certain castle has been erected in the marches between Scotland and England which is called Hermitage.* It is said that Henry then went ahead and used this as an excuse to invade Scotland. The establishment of a stronghold in Liddesdale would certainly have been seen as a threat to England. The castle, like its predecessor would have been built of wood, as stone built castles were a rarity in Scotland until the following century. It may have stood on the site of the present ruins of the castle chapel.

The De Soulis name became one of the most important in Scotland. A Nicholas de Soulis was made Sheriff of Roxburgh in 1248 and he was described as being *the wisest and most eloquent man in the kingdom.* Another Nicholas was one of the claimants to the Scottish throne after the death of Margaret, Maid of Norway and later became a Guardian of the Realm. John de Soulis supported Bruce during the Wars of Independence and died along with Edward Bruce, brother of Robert Bruce, at the battle of Dundalk in Ireland in 1318. John was succeeded by his younger brother, William. It is this William who is usually identified as the wicked Lord Soulis of ballad and legend, though many of the tales surrounding him more properly belong to his ancestor the '*assassinated*' Ranulph.

Legend describes a black magician, steeped in wickedness who came to a nasty end. If it is not historically accurate, it probably reflects attitudes towards the De Soulis family and the dread in which Hermitage was held. It could be that much of the wickedness ascribed to Soulis consisted of a mix of memories and tales from the earlier village of Castletown and which were later transferred to a single person.

According to one of the legends the *Cout of Keelder*, one of Lord Soulis' greatest enemies, was out hunting when he strayed into Liddesdale. Working his evil magic, the wicked lord enticed the young Cout and his followers to Hermitage Castle. Lord Soulis cast a spell on them but he managed to escape as he was protected by a magic helmet. He did not get far though, and drowned in Hermitage after a desperate struggle with De Soulis. men. On the left of the chapel, beside the spot where he is supposed to have met his death, is a mound that tradition says is the grave of the *Cout of Keelder*.

History tells us that in 1290, the Guardians of Scotland ordered Sir William de Soulis, Lord of Liddesdale, to arrest Sir Richard Knout, Sheriff of Cumbria, and bring him to Edinburgh. In order to do this in a lawful manner, it was necessary that Sir Richard be captured on Scottish soil. Less than a year later a document refers to *the late Sir Richard Knout*. We do not know how he met his death but the hill at the foot of the chapel was long known as the Deer Park, so perhaps he was out hunting. The grave of the Cout measured some ten feet in length, a visitor remarked on it to the local grave-digger who told him, *Ah, weel 'e ken, it's the Cout's, an as he was a very big man aw pit other twae feet tae it masel*. So do legends grow.

Over the centuries stories about the wickedness of Lord Soulis grew in the fertile ground of local lore. He mistreated his peasants and terrorised his neighbours. He decoyed the Laird of Mangerton to Hermitage and after entertaining him to a feast, had him cruelly murdered. This deed was made all the more shocking as Mangerton had previously saved the life of his ungrateful lord. Aiding and abetting him in all this wickedness was his accomplice, Red Ringan, who faithfully carried out his master's commands. According to one ballad, their downfall came about when De Soulis abducted a young girl who was promised to the Laird of Branxholm. In order to forestall any opposition, Red Ringan was sent to capture Branxholm Tower and bring the young laird prisoner to Hermitage. Red Ringan succeeded in capturing the laird but failed to capture the tower. Branxholm's brother, Walter the Bold, assembled a large band of men and attacked Hermitage. They captured the castle, rescued the prisoners and took De Soulis prisoner. He was than taken out to Nine Stane Rig where he was boiled alive in a cauldron after being encased in a sheet of lead. It is said that the cauldron had been prepared for some time and that the justification for such a barbaric act had come from the king himself. Growing weary of the constant complaints of De Soulis' tenants, he had exclaimed *Boil him if you please, but let me hear no more of him!*

History tells the story a little differently. In 1320 King Robert I arrested William de Soulis for taking part in a conspiracy to replace him on the throne. When he was arrested, De Soulis was accompanied by over three hundred retainers, all wearing the De Soulis livery. The details of the conspiracy are obscure, but a number of the Scottish nobility were unhappy with the distribution of land after Bruce's victory. De Soulis was the leader of one of the most powerful families in feudal Scotland and may still have harboured ambitions for the crown. He was imprisoned in Dumbarton Castle, while some of his fellow conspirators were put to death. He presumably died there and the name De Soulis does not appear in the pages of Scottish history again. Resentment against the family was given full rein, helped no doubt by the Bruce propaganda machine. It would not make a fitting end if the *wicked Lord Soulis* were allowed to die an ordinary death. Besides they had Nine Stane Rig, a Neolithic circle situated on a windswept moor and for long associated with pagan and magic ceremonies. Desolate and wild, it was a perfect setting for a barbaric and heathen act of communal vengeance. It is on record that a sheriff in the Mearns was boiled alive in a cauldron in the reign of James I. Perhaps this incident was transferred to the De Soulis legend with a little local colour added. There could also be echoes of the assassination of Ranulph de Soulis by his 'domestics' in 1207. Folk memories were long in these days, even if they did get a bit mixed up.

Whatever the truth, Hermitage was regarded with dread by the local peasantry for centuries. Sir Walter Scott often visited the castle. It was one his favourite places where he described the locals as:

Glowrin' roun wi' anxious care
Lest Redcap catch them unaware

Redcap or Redcomb or sometimes Bloody Cap, was a malignant being who was supposed to lurk in ruins associated with evil deeds. Perhaps he is Red Ringan, Lord Soulis' wicked accomplice. He is described as being short and thickset, with long prominent teeth, talon-like fingers, and eyes of fiery red and with long hair that streamed down his shoulders. He carried a pikestaff and wore a red cap on his head. A description detailed enough to keep the most reckless of bairns from the castle ruins.

When De Soulis was being led away to his grisly end, he is supposed to have flung his key over his shoulder saying it would remain where it fell until he returned. In 1806 the Duke of Buccleuch was supervising labourers working in the ruins of Hermitage when they uncovered the remains of a beautiful floor and discovered an old rusty key. There was no doubt in the minds of the workmen to whom the key belonged.

The castle continued to be a centre of strife and bloodshed throughout most of the 14th century. In 1335, Edward Balliol, who was trying to regain the Scottish crown for his family, granted it to Ralph Neville, one of his English supporters. Sir William Douglas captured it in 1338 after having destroyed an English supply column outside Melrose. A grateful monarch rewarded him with Liddesdale and made him warden of the Middle Marches and Sheriff of Teviotdale. However this gallant knight was later to be accused of treasonable correspondence with the English and removed from his offices. These were given to his old comrade in arms Sir Alexander Ramsay, who had recently taken Roxburgh Castle from the English. The Sheriff's post was a particularly lucrative one as he could appropriate all the court fines. Sir William was particularly resentful of this loss and led a force to Hawick where the new sheriff was holding court. He surrounded the courthouse and in the resulting melee wounded Sir Alexander and carried him off to Hermitage. There the unfortunate knight was flung into a dungeon and left to starve to death. Local tradition says that he extended his agony for some days by eating seventeen ears of corn that had fallen through cracks in the floor from the corn loft above his cell. The exactness of the number of ears of corn should make us a bit sceptical of this story and the fact that the room above the cell was actually a guardroom should make us even more doubtful. Sir William was too powerful for the king to bring to justice and no doubt such acts seem more horrific to our sensibilities than they would have been to those of a more violent age. More serious in the eyes of the crown was that the noble knight was once again plotting with the English. This time he was going to allow them free passage through Liddesdale to invade Scotland. In 1352 he was murdered by his nephew while out hunting in the Ettrick Forest. The nephew was granted Liddesdale by a grateful monarch and subsequently became the first Earl of Douglas. He had to wait for a while before he was to enjoy the fruits of his murderous assignment in the Ettrick Forest. The widow of the Knight of Liddesdale appealed to Edward III of England who was trying to consolidate his hold over southern Scotland; loyalty to the Scottish throne was not as strong as self-interest as a motivating factor among the Border nobility. Edward granted her claim to Hermitage on condition that she married an Englishman. Thus encouraged, she promptly married Lord Dacre who seized Hermitage and held on to it until about 1365.

It was during this period of English occupation that the oldest surviving parts of the castle were constructed along the lines of an English fortified house. The castle was eventually recaptured by the Douglases and held by them until 1491. It was further strengthened and extended during this time taking on the aspects with which we are familiar today. The strategic significance of Hermitage in these turbulent times was emphasised when Earl Archibald Douglas was suspected of treasonable correspondence with the English and removed from his post of Guardian of Hermitage. He would not have helped his cause when he murdered Patrick Spens of Kilspindie who was a particular favourite of the king. Hermitage thus came under the control of Patrick Hepburn, Earl of Bothwell. This Earl proved to be equally suspect in his dealings with England. In 1538 the castle was taken over by the crown and made the principal seat of the Warden of Liddesdale with a standing garrison of one hundred men.

It is hardly surprising that the people of Liddesdale should have developed a reputation for thievery and savagery given their geographical situation and also the examples set by their lords and masters. Liddesdale attracted outlaws, criminals and other broken people. Brutalised by violence, cattle rustling and raiding became a way of life. A contemporary remarked, *They have a persuasion that all property is common by the law of nature.* Such was their infamous reputation that they were officially cursed by the Archbishop of Glasgow. Occasionally the Scottish monarch would try to impose his authority on this wild land, he would even allow English armies into Liddesdale to help bring its unruly inhabitants to heel.

The two most powerful families in Liddesdale in the 16th century were the Elliots and the Armstrongs. Owing little or no allegiance to either crown, they raided with impunity in both England and Scotland. In 1566 Mary Queen of Scots travelled to Jedburgh to hold a royal justice court. Her Warden of Liddesdale was the notorious James Hepburn, Earl of Bothwell. He decided to impress the Queen by bringing to Jedburgh some of the Elliots who had been proving particularly troublesome. He found that the hope was easier than the deed. He was stabbed by Little Jock Elliot of the Park whom he had just shot. Elliot was later to die of his wounds but is immortalised forever in the lines:

My name is little Jock Elliot
And wha daw meddle wi' me

The Haunted Borders

The badly wounded Bothwell was carried back to Hermitage but had to negotiate to get back in, as a group of Elliots who had been imprisoned in Hermitage had managed to overthrow the garrison and seize the castle. News of his wounding brought the Queen to Hermitage. Her apparent devotion to the man who was to be the prime suspect in her husband's murder, and whom she later married, was to do her great harm in later years. On her return to Jedburgh, Mary became very ill. So desperate was her condition that her secretary began to make arrangements for her funeral. Years later, during her long imprisonment at Fotheringay castle, she was heard to murmur, *Would that I had died at Jedburgh.* Perhaps Bothwell too was to wish that he could have died at Hermitage when he lay in the Danish dungeon where he was slowly to lose first his mind and then his life. In 1587 the castle came under the control of Francis Hepburn, a young favourite of James VI, who was later made Earl of Bothwell. In time-honoured Border fashion he conspired against his patron and was forced to flee into exile. Hermitage was then granted to Sir Walter Scott of Branxholm in 1594 and remained with the Buccleuch family until 1930, when it passed to the care of the Scottish Development Department.

Its strategic role had disappeared with the Union of the Crowns in 1603 and with it its subsequent role in Scottish history. By the end of the 18th century it had become an abandoned ruin. It was extensively repaired in 1820, but as the plan of the castle before reconstruction had been lost in 1810, it is impossible to know exactly how much the restoration reflected the original structure. The Liddesdale valley became a remote and isolated place. It was not until the 19th century that a road was built to go through it. Much of Scotland's early history is fragmented and hidden from us. Hermitage Castle stands as a gaunt, bleak symbol of dark, disordered times. Perhaps that is why it still has the power to disturb.

Getting There

It is about 16 miles from Hawick to Hermitage Castle. You take the road to Newcastleton. About 4 miles before Newcastleton you turn right. After a few hundred yards Hermitage looms up on your right hand side. It is. guaranteed to take your breath away on first sight. Some people have been known to turn around and go home after this first glimpse.

A few miles further on the road to Newcastleton you take a right turn and a little way up is the site of the original castle of Liddell Crags, part of the remains can still be seen. The original village of Castletown was situated here.

About a mile before the turn-off to Hermitage there is a track off to the left that leads up to Nine Stane Rig.

The Haunted Borders

Site of Kidd's Tower on the hill overlooking the river Liddell

The Curse of the Elliots

The valley of the Liddell and the hills that surround it can be a bleak place in the winter. It is still a relatively isolated spot and it is not surprising to learn that the first wheeled carriage to venture into the wilds of Liddesdale was driven by Sir Walter Scott. Its dark history has been dictated by its geographical situation. Liddesdale is technically part of what was known as the Middle March on the border between England and Scotland but had more in common with the wild Western March. Its importance was recognized by the fact that it justified a warden of its own who was also the Keeper of Hermitage Castle. That sinister edifice

The Haunted Borders

eloquently reflects the grim nature of the valley's history. The ruins and traces of a large number of fortified or peel houses confirm that this was indeed a valley with a violent past. It should not surprise us then that one of the most notorious and predatory of the Border clans had their base in Liddesdale. This was the hard-riding tribe of Elliots.

The origin of the Elliot name and how they came to the Borders is uncertain. There are a number of theories, but the most likely is that they originally came from the village of Ellet near Forfar in Angus and were given land in Liddesdale as a reward for their support of Robert the Bruce. We do know that in 1320 William De Soulis was charged with high treason and imprisoned in Dumbarton Castle. His Liddesdale lands were then divided between Bruce's loyal followers and it is quite possible that the Elliots benefited from the downfall of the De Soulis family. It was not, however, until the latter part of the 15th century that the Elliots emerged as a powerful force in Liddesdale. In 1479 Robert Elwald of Redheuch was given a grant of land by the Liddell and Hermitage waters from the Earl of Angus. A strong peel tower was built at Redheugh and this was to be the home base of the Elliot chieftains. A rental roll for Liddesdale was taken in 1541: there are 46 Elliot families identified along with 34 Armstrongs, 23 Nixons and 13 Crozers. All of them were to develop reputations for thieving and savagery unsurpassed in the wild border country.

Hard times make hard men - and women too. Life in sixteenth century Scotland was always a precarious struggle for the majority of the people. Famine and starvation often followed the failure of the crops, particularly in rural areas, and this was made worse by constant war and invasion. However, it honed down a tough, ruthless and resourceful population for whom personal survival was the key factor in their lives. Protection could not come from royal authority, which was too far away and often too weak to protect those areas on the extreme edges of the realm. It was to their local clan or family chief that people looked for help. Thus there were developed those ties of kinship that overrode all others. A man would follow his chief with no regard for any other consideration. This bond of kinship, while it could provide some sort of protection against outsiders, also encouraged the growth of long, bitter and violent feuds between families that often lasted over several generations. This simply added to the cycle of violence and deprivation that was to create a society made harsh and unforgiving. Pastoral farming was the norm. A man could see a year's hard toil destroyed in an hour if his crop was burned but he had always the chance of driving off cattle to hide them if he was raided. The Elliots of Liddesdale became highly skilled cattle rustlers. From autumn to spring they ranged far and wide, often in bands of more than a hundred riders targeting, in particular, small farmers and lonely steadings where the pickings were good and resistance slight. Of Christian charity there was little. A visitor to Liddesdale remarked on the absence of churches and asked if there were no Christians there. Back came the reply, *Na, na. We's a' Armstrangs an' Elliots.*

It was within this tight, close-knit society that there occurred a tragedy that displays elements of cruelty and of the supernatural that were the hallmarks of so many of the famous Border ballads yet this story never seems to have appeared in ballad form.

A son of one of the Elliot chieftains, Elliot of Larriston, fell in love with Helen Kidd, the daughter of one of his retainers. His feelings were returned and as was the custom of the day they went through a form of trial marriage called handfasting. The handfasted marriage lasted for a year and a day. If at the end of it the couple decided not to continue with it, they parted on amicable terms. The only condition was that any children born from the marriage had to be acknowledged and cared for by the father. Within the prescribed time Helen presented her lover with a son and so delighted was the young Laird that he decided that their marriage should be made permanent and ordered that preparations be made for a wedding.

This caused great consternation among the Liddesdale families. Marriage had always been used as a way of acquiring more land by marrying an heiress or it was a way to strengthen an alliance with another family or clan, very often with one of their Liddesdale neighbours. For a member of the chief's family to marry someone who brought none of these things to a marriage was unthinkable, particularly if she was the daughter of a mere servant. This feeling was shared by many of the daughters of the Liddesdale gentry. They had been casting their eyes at young Larriston, and were enraged and humiliated that he should choose someone as lowborn as Helen Kidd. A handfasted relationship they could tolerate as they assumed that he would grow tired of her and would choose one of them for a more permanent alliance. It was quite unthinkable that they would have to pay her honour if she became the wife of the chief. They started a campaign of slanderous gossip, which they hoped would turn young Elliot against Helen. She was accused of being promiscuous and it was claimed that she had used witchcraft to ensnare the young laird - a very serious accusation in these days. But it was all in vain. The laird laughed off the gossip and named a day for the marriage. The wedding preparations went ahead.

Then, out of the blue, it appeared that the Elliot ladies had a change of heart. Instead of denigrating Helen Kidd they praised her qualities to the young chief. They told him what an excellent choice he had made and how she would make him a fine wife. No doubt the young man was pleased and relieved about this change of attitude. Helen perhaps was more guarded but was persuaded to respond to the Liddesdale ladies, all of whom now seemed anxious to become her friend. They invited her to a pre-wedding entertainment that they had created. We do not know if Helen went to the event with any feelings of foreboding. She ate and drank only to discover that her food and drink had been laced with a powerful poison. As she lay dying she realised how she had been duped and the depth of the Elliot ladies' loathing for her. With her last few breaths, a chronicler writes, *That as her entertainers, the Ladies of Liddesdale, had persecuted her to death for being beloved, so that neither they nor their successors, down to the most distant generation, ever be beloved; might they be doomed to live and die single and solitary, desolate and despised; otherwise, in the event of marriage, might they be doomed to be still more miserable.*

Kidd's Curse, as it came to be known, was long held to be extremely powerful, but perhaps the bleakness of the tale is lightened somewhat by the tradition that the child of Helen Kidd and the young laird became the progenitor of the Elliots of Stobs. Now this takes us out of the realms of local story into that of historical fact. The progenitor of the Elliot Stobs is one Gilbert Elliot known to history as Gibbie w' the gowden garters presumably because of his being regarded as a bit of a dandy in a time and place where even the tiniest adornment to male attire would have been regarded as eccentric, to say the least.

The official history of the Elliots of Stobs states that Gibbie was the third son of Robert Elliot of Redheugh and Jean Scott, a sister of Buccleuch, the chief of the Scotts. However, there is reason to doubt that this was the case. An authoritative source writing of this Gilbert Elliot states, *Of his origin we cannot speak with any degree of certainty, nor do we know what, if any, connection he had with Gavin, his predecessor.* The Gavin referred to here was Gavin Elliot the Laird of Stobs and it is quite possible that he was the grandson of Helen Kidd. It is stated that he was the son of Robert Elliot of Horsliehall who was an illegitimate son of the chief of the clan. This would make Gavin Elliot an older brother of *Gibbie wi' the gowden garters*.

It would also set the time for Helen Kidd's tragic story in the 1530s and confirm that after Helen's death young Robert Elliot did indeed marry Jean Scott in a political marriage that sealed an alliance between the Liddesdale Elliots and the Buccleuch Scotts. It was not to last, for shortly afterwards a bitter feud broke out between the Scott and the Elliot clans.

The Elliots are still numerous in Liddesdale and throughout the Border counties. I am not aware if there are great numbers of Elliot spinsters or that there is a greater number of unhappy Elliot marriages. It is not all that long ago though that an elderly man, on being told that an Elliot girl of his acquaintance was about to be married, shook his head sagely and murmured, *Ay poor thing, nae doot she expects to be happy, but she forgets that Helen Kidd's curse is still clinging to her and her kind to this day.*

Getting There

From Hawick, take the B6399 road to Newcastleton. You will soon be deep in Elliot country. About a mile after you have passed the turn-off to Hermitage, you turn left up the Steel Road. Turn left, at the end of the road, on to the B6357. About a mile up this road you will see Larriston Farm on your right-hand side. The site of the old tower of Larriston is up on the fells beyond the house and farm. There is no trace of the tower to be seen. Continue up this road until you come to Saughtree. On the right-hand side there is a house, which was the old Saughtree school. Below the house is the Liddell. On the opposite bank, about two hundred yards further on, is the site of Kidd's Tower where the unfortunate Helen Kidd lived and possibly died.

The Haunted Borders

Ousenam Water

The Outlaw of Oxnam Water

Robert Burns' contribution to world literature is well known and has been examined and praised in a variety of languages far removed from the Doric of his native Ayrshire. It is often overlooked, however, that Burns made another important contribution to Scottish literature and music. He helped save many of the old Scottish tunes and stories from being lost. In a society where oral tradition was important and where there was little reading or writing, songs and stories were handed down by word of mouth. In earlier days the bards who composed music and the tales were held in high esteem at the King's court and in the baron's hall. Their successors in the middle ages were the wandering minstrels, peddlers and fiddlers who still retained the old tales with which they entertained villagers and farmers.

The Haunted Borders

By Burns' time however, many of the old songs and stories were in danger of being lost forever. They had been forgotten by most of the population as the life and old ways of the countryside started to change due to the seemingly unremitting forces of what were to become known as the agricultural and industrial revolutions. People left their native farms and moved to the towns. The old songs were gradually forgotten as new town-bred generations moved up the social scale, and regarded the old manners of their parents and grandparents with scorn. Their lives moved to different rhythms from those of their forebears. The lack of refinement and the vulgarity of the old Scotch songs did not appeal to the new generation of urban dwellers. It was the women of the country areas who became the transmitters of the old songs and stories. Indeed Burns himself learned much of his Scottish heritage from his mother. Burns was one of a number of people in the late 18th century who realised that a priceless heritage was being lost and set out to recover for posterity as many of the old songs as he could. Of course Burns, like many of his contemporaries, was often guilty of changing the composition to what he felt were more appropriate renditions. Nevertheless, we owe him a debt of gratitude in preserving for us some of the tales and tunes with which we are familiar today.

It was Burns who sent in three verses of *an old and popular song* to Johnson's Musical Museum in 1788.

O rattlin, roarin Willie
O he held to the fair
And for to sell his fiddle,
And buy some other ware

But parting wi' his fiddle
The saut tear blint his ee'
And rattlin roarin' Willie
Ye're welcome hame to me

O Willie come sell your fiddle
O sell your fiddle sae fine,
O Willie come sell your fiddle,
And buy a pint o' wine.

If I should sell my fiddle,
The warld wad think I was mad,
For mony a rantin' day
My fiddle and I hae had.

Burns added a third verse that he had written for his friend William Dunbar who was a fellow member of the Edinburgh social club who called themselves the Crochallan Fencibles. All we can learn from Burns' version of this old song is that it concerned a fiddler who liked a glass of wine and who, no matter how cash-strapped, would never sell his beloved fiddle.

However, over the years a song can change, for it had not been written down and people's memories were somewhat shaky. Often there were several versions of the same song. This is the case with *Rattlin' Roarin' Willie*. But we can, when we look at other versions, begin to get a fuller version of the subject matter. What is important is identifying those parts that are common to the different songs, and, when we do this, a clear tale begins to emerge. This is best illustrated by the version collected by Allan Cunningham in 1825 called *Rob Rool and Rattling Willie:*

The Haunted Borders

Our Willie's away to Jeddart
To dance on the rood-day
A sharp sword by his side
A fiddle to cheer the way
The joyous thairms o' his fiddle
Rob Rule had handled rude,
And Willie left New Mill Banks
Red wat wi' Robin's blude.

Our Willie's away to Jeddart -
May ne'er the saints forbode,
That ever sae merry a fellow
Should gang sae black a road
For Stobs and young Falnash,
They followed him up and down
In the links of Ousenam water
They found him sleeping soun.

Now may the name of Elliot
Be cursed frae firth to firth
He has fettered the gude right hand
That keepit the land in mirth:
And charm'd maids' hearts frae dool;
And sair will they want him Willie,
When birks are bare at Yule

The lasses of Ousenam water
Are rugging and riving their hair
And a' for the sake of Willie
They'll hear his sangs nae mair
Nae mair to his merrie fiddle

Dance Teviot's maidens free:
My curses on their cunning
Wha' gured Sweet Willie dee

So now a clear tale is beginning to emerge of a man whose musical talents made him welcome wherever he went, who killed a fellow bard in a duel and who was subsequently caught and hanged much to the dismay of the Teviotdale maidens. We can also set the story clearly in the Borderland and in particular in the area around Jedburgh. In his introduction to the ballad, Allan Cunningham describes Willie as *a noted ballad-maker and brawler, whose sword-hand was dreaded as much as his bow-hand was admired.*

Sir Walter Scott has set down the details that seem to be known about Willie. He says that he was one of the early Border minstrels who quarrelled with a fellow balladeer, known by the name Sweetmilk. They chanced to meet at an inn at Newmill and resolved to settle their quarrel. They left the inn and crossed the Teviot to an open field. Willie killed his opponent and fled into the woods surrounding Jedburgh near the Oxnam Water. However, Willie grew tired of hiding out in the woods and rashly decided to go in to Jedburgh to enjoy the Rood fair. Unfortunately he was spotted and trailed back to his hiding place by Sir Gilbert Elliot of the Stobs and young Elliot of Falnash. He was handed over to the Sheriff for trial and was speedily condemned and executed at Jedburgh.

These are the bare bones of a tale that was told many times and became changed in the telling. In most cases it becomes impossible to separate out the facts from the legend, but in this case we are fortunate to have a source that confirms the main parts of the oral tradition, the records of the Presbytery of Jedburgh for the year 1628. An entry concerning the parish of Cavers reads:

On the 25th April 1627, the Rev. Walter McGill, minister of the parish, represented to the presbytery that William Henderson, in Priesthaugh (a farm at the base of Skelfhill Pen) parochiner of Cavers had committed a fearful and cruell slaughter in slaying William Elliot called Sweet Milk, quho being summoned and not compeiring, the minister was ordained to caus summon with certification. On May 9 William Henderson being duly summoned compeired not, and the minister was ordained to enter ane process against him. Mr McGill reported to the session that William Henderson had not reported to the Kirk as required neither then nor on the following three weeks. In June the process against William Henderson was renewed but he continued to ignore it. Finally, on the 12 December 1627, the patience of the Session ran out and sentence of excommunication was made against William Henderson along with a number of others.

The sentence of excommunication handed down by the Kirk Session was an important one, for it put William Henderson beyond the law, effectively making him an outlaw. It should be remembered that at this time in Scotland the church, and in particular the Kirk Session was just as powerful and often more effective than the criminal justice system. The civil authorities probably felt that they had insufficient grounds to arrest William Henderson as duelling was looked upon as a legitimate method of settling a dispute in the Borders. The newly established Presbyterian church was to have a long struggle with the state over the boundaries between the authority of the secular government and what they considered to be the *"law of God."* The church had already established that offences including blasphemy and adultery were criminal offences. They wanted this to extend to Sabbath breaking and drunkenness. The church also claimed that *wanton words and licensious living tending to slander do properly appertain to the church to punish the same as God's word commandeth.* The Borders was only just recovering from a long and violent history of bloodshed, feud and social dislocation. The new church was determined to remedy this. If the secular authorities did not act against violent men then the Kirk would. William Henderson was at even greater risk, for the church strongly disapproved of what it referred to as the idle poor, among whose numbers were *Those without lawful calling such as pypers, fiddlers, songsters, somers and strong beggars.* As a noted fiddler and one whose handsome looks had attracted many of the young *Teviotdale maidens*, William Henderson had probably already brought upon himself the strong disapproval of the local Kirk Sessions. In addition the Kirk at this time was trying to cut down on the display and merrymaking at weddings and funerals, occasions at which William Henderson probably earned his living. The Kirk had the power *to excommunicate all impenitents from all sacraments and human intercourse on earth.* In practice, it placed the excommunicant outside the law, together with anyone with whom he had any dealings. If William Henderson had any enemies, he had effectively placed himself in mortal danger.

And William Henderson had enemies, for Sweetmilk was an Elliot, a member of that powerful clan who dominated this part of the Borders. For many years Teviotdale was ripped apart by a feud between the two most powerful families in the area - the Scotts and the Elliots. It is likely that William Henderson was linked to the Scotts. Whether that was true or not, the fact that he had killed an Elliot brought down on his head the full vengeance of that clan. The men who hunted down and captured Willie in the woods beside the Oxnam Water were Sir Gilbert Elliot who rejoiced in the name of *Gibbie wi' the gowden garters* and who was the ancestor of the Elliots of Stobs and the other was Archibald Elliot of Falnash. No doubt many Elliots were members of the Kirk Session that pronounced the sentence of excommunication on the hapless Willie Henderson and probably many of them were also members of the jury who sentenced him to hang. He was to be long remembered though, in the songs and stories about him that were sung and told in Teviotdale and beyond for many years after he departed this life. Old women particularly remembered them in the days of Burns and Scott, who could recall their grandmothers telling them of the handsome young outlaw of Oxnam Water treacherously slain by the vengeful Elliots.

Getting There

The place where Willie Henderson and William Elliot fought their fateful duel was between Branxholm and Newmill about three miles from Hawick on the A7 road to Carlisle. The Rood day fair that was to prove such a fatal temptation to Willie Henderson was held in and around the Market Square of Jedburgh on the 25th of September.

The area where Willie fled and was ultimately captured was the woodland between the Oxnam road and Crailinghall. It is an area marked by deep cleughs and is still heavily wooded. You turn left up the Oxnam road and then a left to Crailinghall. If the spirit of Willie Henderson is still on this earth, then it is here that you will find him. Listen carefully and you may hear the sound of a fiddle playing a merry tune.

The Ballad of Tam Lin

In the latter part of the 19th century the American scholar, Francis J. Child, made it his life's work to collect and classify all the variations of traditional ballads that he could find. These ballads flourished in Scotland, particularly in the 16th and the 17th centuries. The ballads were traditionally sung or spoken and were in great danger of disappearing. Often different versions of a ballad existed and Child tried to make sure that he recorded as many versions of a ballad as possible.

Among the ballads he preserved were several versions of the mysterious *Ballad of Tam Lin*. Version 39 is considered the most authentic and is reproduced here.

Basically a ballad is a song that tells a story. But in order to survive over the generations, the story had to be powerful enough to appeal to changing audiences. The *Ballad of Tam Lin* is a tale that combines the supernatural with a realistic human situation. It is also interesting in that it is consistently placed in the setting of Carterhaugh in Selkirkshire. Sir Walter Scott states in The Minstrelsy, that: *In no part of Scotland, has the belief in fairies maintained its ground with more pertinacity than in Selkirkshire. The most sceptical among the lower ranks only venture to assert, that their appearances, and mischievous exploits, have ceased, or at least become infrequent, since the light of the Gospel was diffused in its purity.* The story is an old one, it is first mentioned in Wedderburn's Complaint of Scotland (1549) but the theme is of much older origin. When Sir Walter refers to the lower ranks, he is referring to the rural Selkirkshire peasantry, among whom pagan and pre-Christian practices continued and Tam Lin is full of pre-Christian symbolism, that would have resonated among the country folk of Selkirkshire.

The story of Tam Lin is about a young man who is a captive of the faeries, and of the Queen of Faeryland in particular. But perhaps the strongest character in the ballad is Janet, the young woman who rescues Tam Lin from the faeries, after he has made her pregnant. It is a story that addresses the nature of courage and the relationship between humans and faeryland. It is worthwhile pointing out that the faeries of Scottish folklore are not the pretty, gossamer winged fairy folk, invented by Victorian writers and artists for children. Our faeries were capricious, occasionally helpful, but always at a cost. They were creatures of the dark and of the deep woodlands who only tended to make themselves known *at the mirk and midnight hour'* There are also vague echoes of an older, pagan memory concerning fertility rituals. In the ballad Tam is a prisoner of the Queen of the Faeries, albeit a not unwilling one, at least up to the time Janet comes to Carterhaugh. He realises that his time with the Queen is coming to an end and that either he is about to lose all his humanity or he is going to be some sort of human sacrifice. In pre-Christian Europe there are accounts of a young male who served as a year king, who was symbolically married to the earth to ensure a plentiful harvest. After the harvest and at the end of the Celtic year the king would be sacrificed. The Faery Queen possesses many aspects of a fertility goddess. Early audiences would have been aware of these links as they listened to the ballad. Tam is the guardian of the faery greenwood and anyone entering without permission had to pay a wad or toll. Now Janet had been expressly forbidden to go to the greenwood, but not only had she gone there but she plucked a rose, which was something akin to damaging faery property. When Tam arrives he demands that she pay her 'wad' or toll. Her payment is to part with her virginity after which she goes back to her father's hall and discovers she is pregnant. For a young unmarried heiress being pregnant is bad enough but to be pregnant to a faery would have been quite breathtaking. However, Janet is a feisty girl and scornfully rejects the offer of getting married to one of her father's knights and is determined to rescue her faery lover and return him to his human state. She is a very bold young lady is Janet, in contrast to Tam who is a passive recipient of both the Faery Queen's and Janet's attentions.

It was important that they got the timing of the rescue right. In the Christian calendar, Hallow'een is the night when ghosts and ghouls have one last fling in the earthly world before being driven off on the morning of All Saints. This was just one among many of the pagan beliefs that were taken over by Christianity. Halloween was originally the Celtic celebration of New Year. For the Celt it was a time to prepare for the approaching winter, a festival to ensure that the sun would return at the end of the winter and it was also the time when the boundaries between living mortals and the past dead and future unborn were blurred and weakened. It was a time of chaos and hope and also great danger. It was a time of great danger for Tam as it would appear that this would have been his last journey and that if he were not rescued that Hallow'een, he would have been lost for ever.

Every story has a first time when it is told, and told in a particular place. Many ballads quickly lost their links to a location or lost the link as the years passed. Practically all the older tellings of Tam Lin come from Scotland and Selkirk in particular. The wood, which Tam protects, is named as Carterhaugh. Carterhaugh is on the peninsula of woods formed where the Ettrick and Yarrow rivers meet in Selkirkshire. Nearby Newark Tower may be the place that, in the ballad, Janet refers to as her father's hall.

Today Carterhaugh on a summer afternoon is peaceful, with little to suggest the dark tale associated with it. But on a bleak November day when the darkening is approaching - well that is another story.

Getting There

Carterhaugh is 2 miles from Selkirk. Turn into the West Port on the A707. Turn left on the B7009. Turn right on to the B7039.

Cross Ettrick Water by a small bridge. Bear right still on the B7039. About half a mile on the left hand side is Tam Lin's Well, though you could miss it rather easily. A few yards further along is Carterhaugh farm.

This is 'Tam Lin Version 39a - written down by Robert Burns.

1. O I forbid you, maidens a'
   That wear gowd on your hair,
   To come or gae by Carterhaugh,
   For young Tam Lin is there.
2. There's nane that gaes by Carterhaugh
   But they leave him a wad,
   Either their rings, or green mantles,
   Or else their maidenhead.
3. Janet has kilted her green kirtle
   A little aboon her knee,
   And she has braided her yellow hair
   A little aboon her bree,
   And she's awa to Carterhaugh
   As fast as she can hie.
4. When she came to Carterhaugh
   Tam Lin was at the well,
   And there she fand his steed standing
   But away was himsel
5. She had na pu'd a double rose,
   A rose but only twa,
   Till upon then started young Tam Lin
   Says, "Lady, thou's pu nae mae

6. "Why pu's thou the rose, Janet,
And why breaks thou the wand?
Or why comes thou to Carterhaugh
Withoutten my command?

7. "Carterhaugh, it is my own
My daddy gave it me,
I'll come and gang by Carterhaugh,
And ask nae leave at thee."

8. Janet has kilted her green kirtle
A little aboon her knee,
And she has snooded her yellow hair
A little aboon her bree,
And she is to her father's ha,
As fast as she can hie.

9. Four and twenty ladies fair
Were playing at the ba,
And out then came the fair Janet,
The flower among them a'.

10. Four and twenty ladies fair
Were playing at the chess
And out then came the fair Janet,
As green as onie glass.

11. Out then spake an auld grey knight,
Lay oer the castle wa,
And says, "Alas, fair Janet, for thee,
But we'll be blamed a'.

12. "Haud your tongue, ye auld face'd knight,
Some ill death may ye die!
Father my bairn on whom I will,
I'll father none on thee."

13. Out then spak her father dear,
    And he spak meek and mild
    "And ever alas, sweet Janet," he says
    I think thou gaest wi child."
14. "If that I gae wi child, father,
    Mysel maun bear the blame,
    There's neer a laird about your ha,
    Shall get the bairn's name.
15. "If my love were an earthly knight,
    As he's an elfin grey,
    I wad na gie my ain true-love
    For nae lord that ye hae.
16. "The steed that my true love rides on
    Is lighter than the wind,
    Wi siller he is shod before,
    Wi burning gowd behind."
17. Janet has kilted her green kirtle
    A little aboon her knee,
    And she has snooded her yellow hair
    A little aboon her bree,
    And she's awa to Carterhaugh
    As fast as she can hie.
18. When she came to Carterhaugh,
    Tam Lin was at the well,
    And there she fand his steed standing
    But away was himsel.
19. She had na pu'd a double rose,
    A rose but only twa

Till up then started young Tam Lin,
Says, "Lady, thou pu's nae mae

20. "Why pu's thou the rose, Janet,
Amang the groves sae green,
And a' to kill the bonny babe
That we gat us between?"

21. "O tell me, tell me, Tam Lin," she says,
"For's sake that died on tree,
If eer ye was in holy chapel,
Or christendom did see?"

22. "Roxbrugh he was my grandfather,
Took me with him to bide
And ance it fell upon a day
That wae did me betide.

23. "And ance it fell upon a day
A cauld day and a snell,
When we were frae the hunting come,
That frae my horse I fell,
The Queen o' Fairies she caught me,
In yon green hill do dwell.

24. "And pleasant is the fairy land,
But, an eerie tale to tell,
Ay at the end of seven years
We pay a tiend to hell,
I am sae fair and fu o flesh
I'm feard it be myself

25. "But the night is Halloween, lady,
    The morn is Hallowday,
    Then win me, win me, an ye will,
    For weel I wat ye may
26. "Just at the mirk and midnight hour
    The fairy folk will ride,
    And they that wad their true-love win,
    At Miles Cross they maun bide."
27. "But how shall I thee ken, Tam Lin,
    Or how my true-love know,
    Amang sa mony unco knights,
    The like I never saw?"
28. "O first let pass the black, lady,
    And syne let pass the brown,
    But quickly run to the milk-white steed,
    Pu ye his rider down.
29. "For I'll ride on the milk-white steed,
    And ay nearest the town,
    Because I was an earthly knight
    They gie me that renown.
30. "My right hand will be gloved, lady,
    My left hand will be bare,
    Cockt up shall my bonnet be
    And kaimed down shall my hair,
    And thae's the takens I gie thee,
    Nae doubt I will be there
31. "They'll turn me in your arms, lady
    Into an esk and adder

The Haunted Borders

> But hold me fast, and fear me not
> I am your bairn's father.

32. "They'll turn me to a bear sae grim,
And then a lion bold,.
But hold me fast, and fear me not,
And ye shall love your child.

33. "Again they'll turn me in your arms
To a red het gaud of airn,
But hold me fast, and fear me not,
I'll do you nae harm.

34. "And last they'll turn me in your arms
Into the burning gleed,
Then throw me into well water,
O throw me in with speed.

35. "And then I'll be your ain true-love
I' ll turn a naked knight,
Then cover me wi your green mantle,
And hide me out o sight."

36. Gloomy, gloomy was the night,
And eerie was the way
As fair Jenny in her green mantle
To Miles Cross she did gae.

37. At the mirk and midnight hour
She heard the bridles sing
She was as glad at that
As any earthly thing

38. First she let the black pass by
And syne she let the brown,

> But quickly she ran to the milk-white steed,
> And pu'd the rider down.

39. Sae weel she minded what he did say,
 And young Tam Lin did win,
 Syne covered him wi her green mantle,
 As blythe's a bird in spring

40. Out then spak the Queen o Fairies,
 Out of a bush o broom,
 "Them that has gotten young Tam Lin
 Has gotten a stately-groom."

41. Out then spak the Queen o Fairies,
 And an angry woman was she,
 "Shame betide her ill-far'd face,
 And an ill death may she die
 For she's taen awa the bonniest knight
 In a' my companie.

42. "But had I kend, Tam Lin," said she,
 "What now this night I see
 I wad hae taen out thy twa grey een,
 And put in twa een o tree."

The Haunted Borders

Tam Lin's Well, Carterhaugh

The Legend of the Linton Worm

The Cheviot Hills form an impressive backdrop to the tranquil beauty of the Roxburghshire parish of Linton. From the knoll on which the ancient kirk of Linton stands, a plain of cultivated fields spreads out towards the village of Morebattle. Little seems to disturb the peace of centuries; an occasional low-flying aircraft or the distant throb of a tractor are the only reminders that we are now in the 21st century. Linton, however, has something other than peaceful scenery to make it a place to be remembered. It is a place associated with a sinister tale of terror and destruction. This is the place that gave rise to the legend of the Linton Worm.

Above the doorway of the church there is a stone with an ancient carving. Time and the Scottish weather have not been kind to the carving much of which has deteriorated. However, a close study reveals a knight on horseback wearing a tunic and a round helmet. He is fighting what appear to be two large animals of which only the foreparts can be made out. The outline of a lamb can also be traced. At one time the following verse is supposed to have accompanied the carving:

The wode laird of Larriston
Slew the worme of Wormiston
And wan aa Linton parochine.

According to the legend, an enormous worm had its den in a hollow to the east of Linton Hill, long after known as Wormshole. From its lair, it ranged across the surrounding countryside destroying everything that lay in its path and killing, with its poisonous breath, all who dared to approach it. The monster created such fear that even the citizens of Jedburgh, ten miles distant, were filled with such panic that they prepared to abandon their town.

All attempts to rid the land of the beast ended in death and failure. Ordinary weapons were of no avail against the giant worm. Just when the sense of despair in the countryside was at its height along came the Laird of Larriston, described as a man of reckless bravery. Fixing a peat dipped in burning pitch to the end of his lance, he charged at the monster and thrust the weapon down its throat. The blazing pitch choked and suffocated the beast, preventing its poisonous breath from killing the brave knight. For delivering the inhabitants from the great worm, a grateful monarch rewarded the Laird of Larriston with a grant of lands in and around Linton. Such is the legend of the Worm of Linton.

Tradition states that the Laird of Larriston was a John Somerville who received the Barony of Linton as a reward for the slaying of the monster. In order to commemorate this the Somerville family has a dragon on the crest of its coat of arms.

History tells us that John Somervill, a baron of Norman descent, who had come north from England, was granted the lands of Linton in 1174. It is also recorded that a Roger Sumerville of Whichenour joined a rebellion against King John of England and had to flee to Scotland in 1214. Roger died in the toure of Linton at the age of 94 - an extremely advanced age for the times.

It will not have escaped your notice that the worm of the legend has been transformed into a dragon on the crest of the Somervilles, an indication of the fact that the exact nature of the beast that so threatened Linton was not entirely clear. In The Memoirs of the Sommervilles, written at the end of the 17th century, the monster is actually described. It is stated to have been *in length three Scots yards, and somewhat bigger than an ordinary man's leg, with a head more proportionable to its length than greatness, in form and colour like to our muir adders.*

Sir Walter Scott suggested that the woods and bogs in the Linton area were infested with exceptionally large serpents. Another theory was that the monster was a very large wolf or boar. This would certainly move the legend back to an earlier period. A mounted and armoured Norman knight could hardly have expected such a reward for killing a wolf or boar, no matter how large.

It is worth bearing in mind, however, that there was no need for a Norman knight to perform a heroic deed to acquire land, for David I and his successors were very keen to encourage Norman knights into Scotland with grants of land. It is possible that at some point in the past the district had been oppressed by an ill-defined evil from which it had been rescued and which was only vaguely remembered as the tale became distorted in the telling down the generations. If this were the case then it would have been well before the Somervilles' time. In the 12th century the Borders was a well-populated and prosperous area, with several richly endowed monasteries and abbeys including Jedburgh and Kelso. Contemporary with the deed that was apparently to bring such benefits to the Somervilles, the monks of Melrose were chronicling the events of the day, but they make no mention of any great calamity that had befallen the district.

The original population of Linton would have been of Celtic stock, but by the 12th century they would have been joined with the descendants of Norse and Anglo-Saxon invaders. The Norse word ormr and the Anglo-Saxon vyrm or wrym can mean either a serpent or a dragon. Legends about dragons are not uncommon throughout the north of England, as indeed are legends about giant worms. The details surrounding the tale of the Linton Worm are very similar to the dragon-slaying stories of tradition, and it is highly probable that the changes in language led to the Linton monster being called a worm when it should really have been a dragon. Legends of dragons are found throughout the mythology of the ancient world, the most famous in the English-speaking world being that of the legend of St George and the dragon, an allegorical description of the triumph of good over evil, more particularly, the triumph of Christianity over paganism.

Memories of paganism would still have been strong in 12th century Linton, for Christianity took a long time to be established in an area where a strong undercurrent of paganism remained within a mixed Norse, Anglo-Saxon and Celtic culture. It was the practice of the early Christian missionaries to erect their churches on the sites of pagan places of worship, thus capitalising on the feelings of reverence and awe that these spots possessed for local inhabitants.

The old gods were cast out and new building rededicated in a Christian manner. That this was the case with Linton Kirk is highly probable. The hill on which the church stands is a prominent and peculiar landmark. It would have been the ideal site for a temple, for the pagan Celts tended to worship on the tops of hills. Most pagan places of worship had a sacred well nearby where sacrificial victims were ritually cleansed. The early church often adopted these sacred wells, rededicating them to the Virgin Mary or Our Lady. Not far to the east of the hill on which the church stands is the Ladywell.

As in other parts of the land, the final triumph of Christianity over the forces of heathenism must have been long and bloody. Added to this, was the fact that the Christian church was the persistent victim of terrifying attacks by Viking raiders who placed the dragon symbol on the prows of their feared dragon ships. By the end of the Viking era, the dragon had come to symbolise forces of evil and heathenism, so that the victory of Christianity over paganism was often represented pictorially through the slaying of a dragon by a Christian hero.

Similar representations have been found in churches in Germany and Scandinavia, but the Linton carving is unique in this country. The manner of the slaying - the lance thrust down the throat - is a common motif throughout all dragon-killing tales. It would appear that the story of the Linton Worm is a Christian myth artistically represented by the carving on the stone.

Symbolic interpretations would not have appealed to the imaginations of the local people as they sought an explanation for the extraordinary carving above their church door, and they perhaps drew from a reservoir of Anglo-Saxon and Norse tales to give it a local colouring. It is perhaps a case of the monument providing the source for the story, rather than the story for the monument, but it is a no less fascinating story for that.

Getting There

Linton is about 8 miles from Kelso. You take the B6352 road to Yetholm. After leaving Kelso you take the first road on your right, the B6436 (you will see Lloyds Agricultural machinery yard on the left hand side). You are now on the Morebattle road. Continue along this road until you come to Linton that consists of only a few houses. Having passed these you will see a small lane on your right. Linton Church is about 150 yards down this lane. The church is situated on a knoll on your right while on the other side is the former manse house. As you will see when you climb up to the church the soil is very sandy. Legend has it that two sisters built it up grain by grain to atone for their brother's crime in murdering a churchman. The carving above the door enclosed to protect it from the ravages of the Scottish weather and is now very indistinct.

A Selkirk Ghost Story

Selkirk in the early years of the 18th century was a bit of a backwater. With a population of around 700 it was a very self-contained community that had changed little over the centuries. Houses were thatched with straw and earth, stables and outhouses for animals were built on to the sides. Like most Scottish burghs it was not a particularly healthy place in which to live and bring up children. Indeed, an early population survey reveals that there were very few children per family, particularly amongst the poorest group, suggesting that child mortality rates were very high. Middens and household rubbish were stacked up against the sides of the houses or thrown on to the streets while pigs were allowed to root about the unpaved wynds and passages. Lack of clean water was a major problem and an early record states that *yearly there is a great sickness in the place and the death of a great many inhabitants."*

The most important trade was that of leather working and in particular the making of a sheen or shoon, which was a type of brogue with a thin sole. The addition of a thick leather sole could be made if the customer was willing to pay. So important was this craft to the economy of Selkirk that the name souter came to describe anyone who was a native of Selkirk. An indication of the importance of shoemaking was the fact that in 1745, despite the fact that the craft was in decline, they still furnished the ragged Jacobite army with over half of the brogues that army had demanded from Edinburgh Town Council.

A very strange tale emerged from Selkirk at this time and it has remained in the collective memory ever since. It has been described by a 19th century commentator as remarkably true story, though it has no doubt gathered a few additions through the years. It concerns one Rab Henspeckle who was a shoemaker living and working in Selkirk's Kirk Wynd probably in the early years of the 18th century. The name Henspeckle is not one that you will find in any of the Selkirk records, nor indeed will you find it in any of the Scottish records. It is what we would now call a by-name or nick-name, probably to differentiate him from many of the other men who shared his real surname. It is also an odd sort of word; henspeckle is not a word that has come down to us but kenspeckle is an old Scots word meaning familiar or well-known. It is possible that henspeckle was originally kenspeckle and referred to Rab the shoemaker who was a familiar figure to all the inhabitants of Selkirk. This probably made his subsequent fate all the more shocking.

The Kirk Wynd, where Rab lived and worked, ran alongside the old St Mary's Kirk. Indeed, the houses on the west side of the street backed on to the churchyard and the minister was constantly complaining about the fact that the inhabitants of the Wynd were in the habit of dumping household rubbish in the kirk yard. He was also not happy with the fact that some of the householders would allow kirk goers to enter the churchyard by going through their houses, thus avoiding paying their collection at the gate. St Mary's Kirk itself was very old; the building with which Rab would have been familiar had been built in 1512 and was in a pretty run-down condition. In 1747 it was to be demolished and a new one built in its place. Few, in that superstition ridden time, would have ventured anywhere near it after dark and if the inhabitants of Kirk Wynd heard noises coming from the kirk yard, they simply pulled their blankets around their ears and ignored them.

Living in such close proximity to the dead did not appear to bother Rab however. He was good at his trade and was known by everyone in the little burgh. He also knew everything that went on in Selkirk for Rab was undoubtedly the most inquisitive man in the town. When he was not working he would be wandering around the streets, noting what was happening and absorbing and passing on the latest gossip. His thin, meagre appearance was well known around the town and it was said that he could tell you what the minister had for his dinner that day and that he knew each of the pigs who snorted and rooted their way through the filthy streets and wynds. His wife found these daily wanderings quite exasperating and had tried vainly to get him to concentrate on his work. It was all to no avail; Rab would make up for the lost time by rising well before dawn to start his daily tasks.

One morning, when there was still a deep darkness outside, Rab was working away on a pair of shoes for the local exciseman. He was bent over, concentrating on the task in hand, when he suddenly became aware that someone was in the room. He looked up and there, standing in front of him, was a tall figure in a large black cloak wearing a broad brimmed hat. Rab was startled for it was very rare to have someone in his shop at that time in the morning. He was even more taken aback as his visitor was a stranger to him and for someone like Rab, who would have been aware of anyone visiting the small town, this was quite disconcerting. Rab had also thought that his door had been locked but assumed that he must have been mistaken. He mentioned to the stranger that it was an early hour to be about in the hope of starting a conversation that would reveal who this mysterious individual was. The man made no response and picked up one of the shoes that Rab had just finished, put it on his foot and walked about the workshop. He turned to Rab, took a rather mouldy smelling purse from underneath his cloak, extracted a gold piece and indicated to Rab that he wanted the other shoe. Rab protested that these shoes were for a customer who was to collect them that day and that he could not possibly sell them to the stranger. Besides he was rather irritated but at the same time intrigued by the stranger's odd manner. The man stamped his feet in anger and Rab hurriedly went on to say that he could have another pair ready for him within twenty-four hours. The man nodded and Rab got him to sit down so that he could measure his feet. As he did so it seemed that there was a strange smell of earth coming from the man, a bit like the smell of a ploughman though much stronger. When Rab asked where he would deliver them the stranger replied in a hoarse sort of voice that he would collect the shoes before cockcrow. Despite all of Rab's chatter, the man said not another word and when Rab had finished his measurements he turned around and strode out. Rab was astonished. He ran to the door and looked up and down the street but the man was nowhere to be seen. He ran down the wynd to the Market Square but it was deserted. He went up the wynd to the churchyard at the end but, as a grey and murky dawn emerged, all he saw were the rows of silent, grey gravestones. He scratched his head under the red nightcap that he had neglected to remove when he got up and swore to himself that he would find out who the stranger was that day, even if it was to kill him.

For the rest of the day Rab worked on the shoes. His wife was astonished and neighbours shook their heads in amazement for never before had Rab neglected his daily wanderings for work. But Rab was a man obsessed: he had to find out who the stranger was, particularly as everyone insisted that no visitors had come into Selkirk the previous day. That night he could not sleep and was up well before dawn with the finished shoes. As soon as he heard the cock crow he flung open his door and peered out into the darkened wynd. From out of the shadows a hoarse and gravelly voice said, *Where are my shoes?* Startled, Rab ushered him into his workroom where the man sat down and tried on the shoes. Evidently satisfied he drew out a gold coin from under his cloak

The Haunted Borders

and left without saying another word. Once again Rab noticed that strong earthy smell the stranger left behind him.

Rab darted to the door. The man was walking slowly with a heavy dragging gait, making it easy for Rab to follow him. The stranger turned into the kirkyard. Rab followed and saw the man sit down on a grave for what Rab assumed was a rest. Somewhere a crow cawed. Rab glanced up and when he looked back at the churchyard the man had disappeared. Thoroughly shaken Rab still had the presence of mind to place a large stone on the grave to act as a marker so he could identify it later. He then hurried home to relate all that had happened to his sleepy wife.

The story of Rab Henspeckle's strange encounter spread rapidly throughout the town. It caused great consternation, for witchcraft, ghosts and spirits were accepted as real but terrifying features of life and this situation had to be tackled before it got out of hand. It was decided to go to the kirkyard and open the grave. All of the folk of Kirk Wynd turned out to watch a group of eminent burgesses scrabble at the earth. The corpse was uncovered and there on its bony feet was a pair of new shoes that Rab immediately identified as his. This was all too much for many of the spectators who fled back to their homes overcome with terror at what kind of evil had been uncovered. Only Rab and a few of the more stern-minded burgesses remained. It was decided that the best thing to do was to dig a deeper hole in which to bury the corpse. This was done and the body was placed in it. Just before the first sods of earth were flung in Rab jumped down and removed the shoes saying there was no point in leaving a good pair of shoes with someone who did not need them. The burgesses looked at each other but said nothing and continued with the burying of the corpse.

When darkness came few people ventured out, still affected by the strange events of the day. The next morning, however, Rab was up before dawn as usual working away and singing to himself. Next door his wife, who was still in bed, was awakened when Rab's singing changed to cries of terror. She gripped the blankets as she heard the sound of a short struggle followed by silence. She got up and ran into the workshop. Rab's stool was lying broken on its side and the door was wide open. There had been a light fall of snow and she was able to follow a set of footprints from the door into the kirkyard. She raised the alarm and once again in the early morning light the group of burgesses stood over the grave that they had exhumed the day before. Once again they dug up the grave and once again they uncovered the skeletoid corpse. Rab's shoes were once again on its feet. In its bony hands it clutched Rab's red nightcap but of Rab Henspeckle there was no sign. He was never to be seen in Selkirk again.

Getting There

The Kirk Wynd runs from the Market Square in Selkirk up to the A7. It is a very different street to the one that Rab Henspeckle would have remembered. It is very wide compared to the alley that it would have been in his time. To get an idea of what it would have been like, you should walk up the wynd in which the Halliwell House Museum is situated. St Mary's Kirk yard is still situated on Kirk Wynd where the remains of the ancient church can be seen. And if you are there when the darkening is descending and an emaciated looking individual comes up and asks you what you are doing, try and find out his real name - before you run off!

St Mary's Kirk, Selkirk

The Haunted Hills

And if you watch by Eildon
The Eildon Hills are three
When twilight shadows deepen
Then strange things you will see

The Eildon hills are such a familiar part of the Borders landscape that it is impossible to imagine the Borderland without them. There are few places from where their triple peaks cannot be seen. Walkers on other Border hills have for centuries used them to get their bearings and for the traveller coming home from the south they must have been a welcoming sight. From the top of Eildon Hill North you can gaze out over the Borderland and from there, Sir Walter Scott claimed he could identify forty-three locations associated with the area's lore and legend.

They are in fact three hundred and fifty million years old. Formed of volcanic rock when the world was still young, they have seen the rise and fall of the dinosaur and watched and survived the onset of the Ice Age glaciers that covered the Borders for over a million years.

As the ice retreated, they observed the bleak tundra left behind gradually develop a carpet of shrub and forest. About fifteen thousand years ago small groups of hunters and food-gatherers paddled up the river valleys in pursuit of wild animals in the surrounding forests. Later their ancestors were to discover the art of farming and they were to clear the woods around the hills to make room for the planting of crops and the creation of pastureland for their animals. And all the while the triple peaks of the Eildons held for them a kind of wonder as well as providing a vantage point from which they could survey the whole of the vast forest laid out before them. Such strangely shaped hills would always have exerted a fascination for the early hunters and farmers who came into the area. High places were associated with the supernatural and so were the Eildons. We do not know very much about the ceremonies and beliefs of those early inhabitants of the Borders but their rites and rituals would probably have been based around hunting and animals. Successive waves of incomers absorbed the original population together with many of their beliefs which may still live in local folklore and superstitions, the origins of which we are unable to identify.

It was the Celts who were to leave a substantial mark both physically and spiritually on the Eildon Hills. The remains of the large hill fort on Eildon Hill North shows that it was as important a settlement as that on Traprain Law in what is now East Lothian. Up to two hundred and sixty outlines of houses or huts have been traced but it is unlikely that it was a permanent settlement. It may have been resorted to at times of attack or used for gatherings or festivals. Festivals were particularly important to our Celtic forebears. They were a people who believed that the natural world and that of the supernatural were closely intertwined. Rituals had to be followed closely in order that the forces from the Otherworld did not harm mortal people. There was a kind of pagan priesthood who acted as the link between this world and the next and who exercised a great deal of authority through their ability to read the future and act as intermediaries with a whole host of pagan gods. The number three had great significance to this priestly cult, whom some have identified as the Druids to whom Julius Caesar referred in his account of the invasion of Britain. The triple-peaked Eildon Hills must have therefore assumed great significance for them in the practice of their secret rites. There are a number of springs at the foot of the Eildons that were later given the names of Christian saints. It was common practice for the early church to give such names to wells that had been venerated by the pagans. The spirits of rivers and springs were particularly powerful deities to whom the Celts made frequent offerings and there is some of this in the Eildons. The reputation of the Eildons as a place of worship and sacrifice was retained for a long time in folk-memory. On the north side of the middle hill, near the foot, there is a little hill known as *"The Bourjo"*. It was said that pagan priests performed their ceremonies here in an oak grove. For centuries afterwards the place was regarded with a mixture of fear and dread.

One of the greatest and most important of the Celtic festivals that would have been held here was the ancient and dreaded festival of Samain. It marked the end of one pastoral year and the start

The Haunted Borders

of another and was held on the 31 October every year. It was a time when the Otherworld became visible to mankind, when the forces of the supernatural were let loose upon the earth. It was also a time of great danger. The brotherhood of priests had to offer sacrifices to propitiate the forces of the Otherworld and the ceremonies had to follow the exact ritual that had been laid down for centuries. Whether human sacrifices were made is a point of conjecture. What is certain is that at times of crisis or when the Otherworld seemed about to overwhelm the people, then appropriate and significant sacrifices had to be made. That the hills were a place of pagan ritual is incontrovertible but we can only guess at the nature of these rituals.

Romans came and established their most important base in Scotland at the foot of the Eildons. The road that they built led unerringly to the base of the hills from which their camp took its name. Trimontium - the place of the three hills - was to be a frontier town for almost four hundred years. The surrounding tribes were forced to exist peacefully, if not happily, under Roman protection. The territory of the two local tribes, the Votadini and the Selgovae, became a sort of buffer state between the Roman Empire and the wild Caledonian tribesmen of the north. The departure of the Romans in 410 led to a period of upheaval among the Romanised Celts of the area. Waves of invasions from the north and also from the south by advancing Angles were to wreak havoc among the Celtic speakers of the Borders. At the same time the arrival of Christianity, which saw the establishment of a Christian foundation at Melrose at the foot of the Eildons, caused divisions between the native Britons, as we could call them. Some remained true to their pagan ways, while others embraced Christianity. They were thus unable to unite to fight against the greater threat of the Anglian invasion from the south. Though southern Scotland was to be colonised by the Angles and many of the Britons departed to live with their kinsmen in Wales, the memories of the Britons were kept alive in the numerous place-names of the area and in the folklore of the people who came after.

The name that had been given to the hills by the earliest settlers and possibly by their Celtic successors has been lost to us. The name Eildons comes from the old English, with possibly still a trace of Celtic. Its usual derivation is aill - a rock and dun a hill. Another possible interpretation is suggested by the first reference to the hills in the foundation Charter of Kelso Abbey where the hills are referred to as Aeldonam. This, it is claimed, is the Latinised form of the old English words aeled meaning a fire and dun, a hill- the hills of fire. It is just possible that this is a reference to some of the religious festivals that may have been carried out on the top of the hills and were associated with the lighting of midwinter fires.

For many years the Eildon Hills were regarded with supernatural awe. It is not surprising then that the Eildons were the setting for the story of the seduction of Thomas the Rhymer. The story retains many of the elements of Celtic mythology. Thomas fell asleep on the eastern slope of the hill and when he awoke he saw a woman dressed in green standing before him. She was the Queen of the Fairies and was so attracted to Thomas that she took him as her consort to Fairyland which lay under the Eildons where he was to reign with her for seven years. The Celtic fairies were very different from the simpering, gossamer sprites of Victorian fiction. They were marginally smaller than humans and were invariably dressed in green. Although they could be friendly to humans there was always a price to be paid for their help. Being the consort of the Queen, while undoubtedly having its compensations, would exact an unnamed but sinister reckoning and one in the end which Thomas could not avoid paying. While we know that Thomas of Ercildoune was an actual historical character it is not surprising that it is the Eildon Hills that provided the supernatural background to his legend.

The hills continued to be avoided by local people particularly at night. However, in the middle of the 18th century a gypsy horse dealer from Canonbie, known only as Dick, arrived in Melrose with some horses to sell. Dick had a reputation as a womaniser and, unfortunately, was discovered in a compromising position with a local woman by her irate husband. Dick decided that it was time to make a quick departure. Together with his unsold horses he took a hurried leave of Melrose. He had reached a spur on the western side of the hill known as the 'Luckenhare', when it became too dark to continue, so he set up camp for the night. Out of the gloom a figure appeared. It was an old man wearing a cloak and sporting a resplendent white beard. He enquired if Dick's horses were for sale. Dick said they were and, on being offered a very generous price, he quickly agreed to sell them. He was even more delighted when he was paid in gold coin but noted that they were of ancient vintage.

The old man requested that Dick sell him some more horses and that he come back at an agreed time, just before darkness fell, to this same spot. Over the next few months these transactions were carried out several times to Dick's considerable profit. He was, however, intrigued by who the old man was and where he went with his horses. Whenever he had tried to follow the old man and the horses, he always lost them on the dark hillside. Eventually he asked the old man who he was. He replied that he was Thomas of Ercildoune and that if Dick felt brave enough he would show him where the horses were kept. Dick agreed and followed the old man into the gathering gloom. Suddenly they came across an opening in the hillside that Dick had never seen before. On entering he found himself in a huge cavern. Along the sides were rows of knights in black armour, all of whom appeared to be fast asleep and beside each knight stood a black horse. On a table in the middle of the cavern lay a hunting horn and a sword, still in its scabbard. The old man indicated that Dick should pick up one or the other. *Either draw the sword or blow the horn. Choose well and you reign here as king; choose badly and you shall forfeit your life"* Dick paused only for a moment before he picked up the horn, put it to his lips and blew. There was an ear-shattering blast and immediately the sleeping knights leapt up and the horses neighed and pranced. Frantically Dick felt for the sword and on grasping it, pulled it from its scabbard. All was noise and confusion. Dick, needless to say, realised that he had made the wrong choice. The next thing he remembered was waking up on the hillside. No cavern was to be seen. He set off wearily down the hillside and told his story to anyone who would listen. Whether they took him seriously is not recorded, but they did have cause for reflection when Dick died a few days later.

There had long been a legend that a mighty king, along with his men, slept in a deep fairy sleep beneath the Eildon Hills waiting a time when they would all be needed to save their people. Their people would have been these Romanised Britons fighting off the Angles from the south and Pictish and Scottish neighbours from the north. The warrior king lying beneath the Eildons was the fabled King Arthur upon whom the Scottish Borderland has as good a claim as any other part of Britain.

Getting There

If you want to walk on the Eildons, there are several routes you can take. One path can be found by turning off the A68 and taking the A699 road to St. Boswells. You turn right up the B6359. After about a mile you see Bowden Moor Reservoir on your right. You can park here and follow the footpath that takes you past the Lucken Howe on your right where Canonbie Dick had his meeting with Thomas of Ercildoune.

Another route can be found by parking in Melrose square and walking up the B6359. A few yards up on your right-hand side is the footpath that can take you either to Mid Hill or Hill North. Another route is to leave Melrose on the A6091 heading for Newtown St Boswells. You turn right up the old A6091, which is now a "no through' road. You can take a footpath at the end of this road that takes you up Eildon Hill north. At the start of this footpath you will see a stone indicating that this is the supposed site of the tree under which Thomas the Rhymer had his encounter with the Queen of Elfland.

Witchcraze in the Borders

For the first half of the 17th century the Scottish Borders remained a poor, backward and primitive part of Scotland. Long centuries of war, together with frequent famines had left their mark on a brutalised population and a neglected landscape. The Union of the Crowns in 1603 had caused the frontier to disappear but it was to be many years before a social system based on the effective rule of law was to emerge to take the place of rule by terror, bullying and blackmail. Change did not come easily or swiftly. A series of failed harvests in the 1620s brought starvation to many Border towns and villages. The 1640s saw a repetition of the harvest failures. The effects were made worse by the raging Civil War that brought bands of ill-disciplined soldiers rampaging through the countryside. Such poverty does not bring out the best in human beings. Hunger, fear and deprivation combined to create intolerance and suspicion of one's neighbours. It was out of this sad combination of forces that what is sometimes referred to as the witchcraze spread like a pestilence throughout the Borders.

Poverty alone, however, does not explain the sporadic outbursts of witchcraft prosecutions. Nor does it explain why it was so intense in Scotland where more than 3,000 people were executed for witchcraft compared to only 1,000 in England with a population five times as large. Belief in witchcraft and the supernatural was accepted in the 16th century by all classes of society: educated and uneducated, rural and urban. People had recourse to herbalists, often old women who, through their knowledge of herbs and plants, effected cures which often seemed miraculous to the recipient. Similarly the local soothsayer or spae-wife was often consulted with regard to important life-events such as marriage or birth or when best to sow a particular field. That they were in touch with the supernatural was accepted as a normal part of the world. You could keep in with such people by giving them gifts in the same way as milk or food was left out to keep on the good side of the fairies or 'little people.' Everybody in the Borders knew that if you made a cross of rowan twigs tied with red thread above the lintel of your door that this would help keep out witches. *Rowan tree and red thread gar the witches tyre their speed* was a well-known saying in the Borders. The rowan tree is still regarded as a lucky tree and is still planted in the garden of many a new house. The coming of the Reformation had the effect of forcing the new Protestant churches to vigorously establish their moral authority. The worship of saints, leaving food for the fairies and consulting soothsayers became not just superstitions but deadly sins. In similar vein John Calvin, the Protestant theologian, who was to have such a strong influence on the development of Protestantism in Scotland, declared that *God expressly commands that all witches and enchantresses shall be put to death and this law of God is the universal law.* It is not altogether surprising, therefore, that the persecution of witches was most intense in those areas of Scotland where Presbyterianism was strongest. There were few cases in the Highlands where belief in the supernatural was widespread, and a Presbyterian system of church government was weakest.

It is noticeable that in Scotland the landed classes and the wealthier burgesses were seldom accused of witchcraft. It was mainly women who were targeted and these tended to be wives of small farmers or craftsmen or more commonly elderly widows who might be proving to be a burden on the parish funds for the upkeep of the poor. Often it was the local minister and the kirk elders who, sincere in their belief of the existence of the devil and the struggle between good and evil, felt compelled to denounce local women as witches.

They had a framework for the seeking out and identification of witches in the book *'Malleus Mallificorum'* which translated as *'The Hammer of Witches.'* This book was published in Germany and proved popular throughout Europe, though quite fraudulent, it was nevertheless taken up by the church as a textbook on witchcraft. It was from this book that the popular caricature of the witch as an old woman in a cloak and pointed hat entered into common currency. In fact it was the normal dress of elderly

The Haunted Borders

women in Europe at that time. If 'Malleus Mallificorum' gave some kind of spurious intellectual authority to the identification of witches, then the publication of a book by the King himself gave witchcraft persecution an intellectual respectability. In 1597 James Vl published his 'Daemonology' which was taken up by learned men in the kingdom. In it he claimed that witchcraft was essentially part of the devil's conspiracy against the state, and God's appointed rulers like himself. James took a keen interest and became personally involved in the interrogation of suspected witches particularly during the much publicised trial of the North Berwick witches in 1590. Thus, the seeking out of witches was given the royal seal of approval and had the active support of many of the landed gentry.

The Privy Council would often grant commissions to *resident gentlemen and ministers to examine and try witches.* The normal pattern would be that a woman who was suspected of being a witch was denounced and brought to trial. It was necessary, in Scotland, that proof be established before the trial began and ideally this should include a full confession. This was usually forthcoming, for the use of torture to extract confessions was an accepted part of the Scottish judicial process. The victim would also be searched to find a witche's mark, usually a spot on her body that proved insensitive to pain and into which a needle could be plunged. The victims through fear or pain would give names of their supposed accomplices and so other women would be arrested and subjected to the same horrific process. One woman who was named in this way and languished in the jail at Lauder actually pleaded that she be put to death. She stated *As I must make answer to the God of Heaven presently, I declare I am as free of witchcraft as any child, but being delated by a malicious woman and put in prison under the name of a witch, disowned by my husband and friends and seeing no grand hope of my coming out of prison, or ever coming in credit again through the temptation of the devil, I made up that confession on purpose to destroy my own life, being weary of it and choosing rather to die than live.* There is here an inkling of the human tragedy brought about by the malicious gossip of a neighbour. It is undoubtedly the case that you were more at risk from your neighbour than you were from the local authorities.

Many accusations of witchcraft were concerned with a cow ceasing to produce milk, a domestic accident or a sudden illness in the family. All too often it was easy to blame such mishaps on an unpopular or eccentric neighbour. Consider for instance, the list of charges brought against Elizabeth Bathgate who was the wife of Alexander Rae, a maltman in Eyemouth. She was arrested in 1634 on charges of sorcery, being accused by George Sprott of forcibly entering his house and removing some cloth that actually belonged to her. He also claimed that she had cursed his child and gave it an egg that contained a foul charm, after eating the egg the child died. She was also accused of threatening George Sprott and told him that he would never be able to provide for his wife and children, shortly afterwards Sprott fell into dire poverty. No doubt he desperately cast about for some explanation for his ill-fortune. In his anger and despair, he decided to accuse a neighbour with whom he had fallen out of being a witch. As was so often the case, once someone was accused of witchcraft others who had suffered misfortunes also emerged to accuse Elizabeth Bathgate. William Donaldson said that shortly after he had called her a witch he was struck down by an illness that left him a cripple. Margaret Home stated that she had borrowed money to buy a horse and a cow from the accused and both animals died. This seemed to open the floodgates and Elizabeth Bathgate was accused of the sinking of ships, the burning of barns and of causing mysterious illnesses. Elizabeth was probably fortunate that at this time the Scottish judiciary was having qualms of conscience about the use of torture to extract confessions of witchcraft. It could be that she was thus able to avoid having to confess. Whatever the reason Elizabeth Bathgate was one of the very fortunate ones who was actually acquitted of all charges and set free. I would doubt, however, if she and her husband chose to remain in Eyemouth. She is remembered in a piece of doggerel verse that was chanted by children, long after those involved had been forgotten:

She's sunken George Houldie's ship
And drowned all his men and their equip
And with her devilish squad
Has made Tom Burgen's nag rin mad.

Eyemouth and Berwickshire seemed to have been particularly prone to the persecution of witches. In 1594, it was noted that, *This year, in the Merse, there was a great business about sorcery and the trials of witches, and many was there burnt, as, namely, one Roughhead, and Cuthbert Hume's mother of Dunse, the parson of Dunse's wife, and sundry of Eyemouth and Coldingham; near a dozenne, and many fugitives.* A hundred years later Sir Alexander Home of Renton wrote to Lord Polwarth complaining of the great increase in the number of witches in the parish and remarked that his father, as Sheriff, had *caused burn, seven or eight of them.* He was probably referring to eight women from the small village of Auchencrow who were burnt for witchcraft at Coldingham. No details of the charges have come down to us but such an horrific occurrence in such a small community must have made a deep impression particularly on the husbands and children of those put to death. It may well have been they had proved to be troublesome tenants and it was felt that they required to be taught a lesson. Auchencrow was to remain a village with a reputation for witchcraft for many years. Long after the belief in witchcraft was supposed to have died away, an old woman named Margaret Girvan died in her hut on the edge of the village. It was a day of high winds and it was remarked upon by many that it was a well-known fact that when a witch departed this life the wind blew strong. The evil reputation of Auchencrow is remembered in the line of verse:

In Edencraw, where the witches bide a'.

The eastern Borders was the setting for one of the most extraordinary witchcraft cases that took place in Scotland. It was made all the more unusual by the fact that the person accused of being a 'warlock' was John Niell of Tweedmouth. It is a strange tale, which illustrates the fact that belief in witchcraft and sorcery was prevalent throughout all ranks of Scottish society. In 1630 Alexander Hamilton, who was described as a notorious warlock, had, under torture, accused a number of women of being witches. There was nothing unusual about this as it was well known that witches did not operate in isolation and those accused were *encouraged* to name their *accomplices*. What was unusual in this case was that one of the women named was no less a person than Lady Home of Manderston in Berwickshire. Hamilton accused her of having practised witchcraft against her husband, Sir George Home, in an attempt to kill him. Under torture, Hamilton revealed that he had been told about the murder attempt by John Niell who was described by the authorities as, *being long reputed to be ane notorious warlocke and ane practizer of witchcraft*. It was the outraged husband, Sir George Home, who was given a commission to arrest Niell, which he duly carried out and Niell was imprisoned in the tolbooth in Edinburgh while he awaited trial. His trial caused a sensation with a very large number of witnesses called, all of whom came from Berwickshire, including every parish minister. John Niell had obviously upset a lot of people. Indeed, the importance given to the case was shown by the fact that landowners were instructed to make sure that those of their tenants who were called as witnesses turned up at the trial. Among the charges laid against John Niell were *of the takin off and laying on of diseases;* for example he ordered that a sick person's shirt be washed in south running water. He was also accused of holding consultations with the devil on Coldingham heath and of *giving responses concerning the time and manner of people's deaths.* It was said that he planned the death of Sir George Home of Manderston by putting *an enchanted dead foal in Sir George's stable and burying a dead hand enchanted by the devil"* in Sir George's garden. Sir George then succumbed to a serious illness from which he did not recover until the dead foal and the dead hand were discovered and burned. John Niell was found guilty and burned at the stake in Edinburgh. Meanwhile Lady Manderston was accused of *of consulting anent the death and destruction of her husband.* Needless to say she was acquitted. John Niell was probably a confidence trickster who made a good living off the gullibility of people, perhaps he even believed in his powers himself. He inevitably came unstuck when he became involved with the landed gentry and proved no match for them. It was a well-known fact that Lady Manderston and her husband did not get on well. A few months after the trial Sir George was ordered not to molest his wife or any of her tenants, *in their bodies, lands, rooms, possessions, corns, cattle, guids or geir or otherwise nor by order of law.* Bearing in mind that belief in sorcery was held bv all classes of society it is not unlikely that she did seek out John Niell's advice. Within a year of the trial her husband did actually die. Did she, I wonder, give thanks to the hapless John Niell?

It is to be hoped that John Niell was strangled before he was burned as this was was the normal course of action when someone confessed to their crimes. If they proved recalcitrant however, they were *burnt quick*, that is to say that they were burned alive. Such public executions must have had a horrid fascination for the community. The persistence and nature of witchcraft persecution must have resonated with some deep and dark part of the human psyche, into which it might not be wise to look too closely. Certainly the trials must have provided an outlet for the sadistic impulses of some of the prosecutors. But the community too indulged in a great deal of gratuitous cruelty. Meg Lawson was condemned as a witch in Selkirk towards the end of the 17th century. Apparently her jailers were surprised to find the remains of some herring in her cell one morning, when none had been left the night before. They accepted Meg's explanation that during the night she had turned herself into a mouse, gone through a hole and ridden on a broom to Edinburgh and had got the fish there. It was believed that though she had the power to change her shape and leave her cell, she was unable to put off her death and her meeting with her master. Her explanation seemed much more likely than the fact that someone had brought it to her. The next day as she was being dragged to the Gallows Knowe, she begged her guard for some water, *Na, na, he replied, the drier ye are ye'll burn the better.* Meg Lawson left several children and they were to suffer from her reputation. In 1721 the Selkirk Kirk Sessions record that a deacon was reprimanded for accusing John Lukup of being a witch, *one of Meg Lawson's kind,* and that he had *overmuch of his luckie-mother Meg Lawson's airt.* John Lukup's wife was Meg Lawson's daughter. He said that they had been married for twenty-four years and that they had barely *twenty-four hours peace together,* presumably because of persecution by their neighbours.

By the 1660s was illegal to practice 'witch pricking' without a licence from the Privy Council. But it was not until 1736 that the statutes against witchcraft were repealed. This was greeted with outrage by many churchmen who regarded the repeals as contrary' to the express law of God. People's beliefs, however, are not changed as easily as the law. It was a long time before belief in witchcraft was to die down. The number of places known as Witches Knowe serve to remind us of one of the darkest episodes in the history of the Borderland.

The Ghosts of Littledean Tower

Littledean Tower stands in a dramatic situation on the top of a high bank overlooking the river Tweed just outside the village of Maxton. Today Maxton is a sleepy Borders village but at one time it was a large and thriving settlement which, it is said, could raise over a thousand armed men. Littledean has obviously been an important stronghold in its day. It is positioned on a strategic situation overlooking an old ford. Its walls were six feet thick. With a plan that is unique among Scottish castles it is built in the shape of the letter D with the flat part looking out over the Tweed. It was probably built sometime in the early 14th century though the first record of it was in 1525 when a *Marcus Ker of Litil Dene* was mentioned. The tower belonged to a branch of the Kers of

The Haunted Borders

Cessford who appear to have owned it without a break until its abandonment in the mid 18th century, after which it was allowed to fall into ruin. The Kers were major players in the anarchic society of the Borders in the 16th century and Littledean Tower played a major role in that blood-ridden century though only fragments of its history have come down to us. In 1544 it is recorded that the hall and stables were burned down but the stone house escaped because it was mired with earth. The details of what was probably a bloodthirsty history have not come down to us, yet fascinating stories surrounding Littledean Tower survived for a long time in the folk memories of the local people. For them Littledean Tower was a place to be feared for its association with sinister stories of the supernatural.

About half a mile to the east of the village of Maxton there is a burn with a small bridge running across it. In a field nearby, the ghosts of two ladies dressed in white were seen in the evening walking arm in arm. They made their walk that was always in the same place for over a hundred years. About 1882 when workmen were repairing the road beside the burn they lifted up two large flat stones that up to that time were used as stepping-stones to cross the burn. Underneath they found two female skeletons lying side by side. Local tradition says that the ladies were sisters of a Laird of Littledean named Gilles. They apparently tried to prevent him raping a girl he had come across while out walking with his sisters. In his rage and frustration he slew his sisters, threw their bodies in the burn and placed the stone slabs over them. The ghostly ladies were never seen again after their bones had been reburied.

It would appear to have been this same laird who was to be the subject of a well-known story surrounding Littledean Tower. Certainly he shares much of the same traits as the one who had so horribly disposed of his sisters. Curiously he is referred to as Gilles but as there is no such name on record as being associated with Littledean we must assume he was a Ker, as they owned Littledean without a break down to the 18th century. It may well be that when the tale was told around winter fireside that the name was changed so as not to offend the powerful Ker family who still held the future prosperity, if not the lives, of many families in their ruthless hands.

The Laird of Littledean was described as tall, dark, very handsome and very wicked. He lusted after the local girls and treated his servants very badly; indeed, it was said that he had caused the death of a stable boy. So low had his reputation sunk that only people with the same tastes as himself came to the wild parties he loved to hold in the tower. His wife, Margaret, was of a pious disposition. She resorted to prayer to try to make her husband mend his errant ways but it was to no avail. At one of his parties the drunken laird was taunted by one of his guests as to why his wife never attended his parties. He demanded that she come down and greet his guests. When Margaret refused, the Laird pulled her down and struck her which shocked even that hardened company. *I'd rather be wed to a fiend from hell than to you,* he roared at her. *At least she'd have more warmth about her.* Margaret raised herself from the floor, fixed her eyes on him and said slowly, *you will live to regret those words.* She got up and walked out of the hall. By this time the assembled company had crept away in a rather shamefaced fashion leaving the Laird slumped in a chair cursing softly to himself. He continued to drink heavily. Eventually he staggered to his feet and called for his horse. His servants probably thought that this was not too good an idea but as their master rarely listened to them when he was sober, it was even less likely that he would listen to them when he was drunk. No doubt some of them hoped that he would break his neck. Still cursing the laird galloped off into the darkness. He rode far into the night without regard to where he was going. Suddenly a storm came up and torrential rain poured down. The laird took his horse into a small wood. Through the dripping trees he spied a small clearing with a rather poor looking cottage at the far end. He made his way towards it, pushed open the flimsy door and went in. A woman was sitting at a spinning wheel with her back towards him. He stood for a moment or two, accustoming his eyes to the dim light. The woman turned towards him. He gasped with a mixture of astonishment and growing lust. The woman was dark haired and beautiful with bold laughing eyes full of what he interpreted as mischief. The rain had stopped and his horse moved restlessly outside. The woman's eyes held the Laird's gaze. Suddenly a coldness swept over him and sobriety returned. A voice inside him told him to return to the tower for he had some early business to attend to. He continued to stare at the woman who took a strand of the thread she had been spinning and snapped it in two with her white teeth, all the time looking into his eyes, a smile playing at the corner of her mouth. A mixture of lust and something more that he could not define made him want to stay. At the same time he felt a cold feeling of fear at the strangeness of this encounter. Fear and his need to return to the tower overcame desire. He turned, mounted his horse and rode back to Littledean.

In the days and weeks that followed he could not get the woman out of his mind. He hunted for the small wood and cottage but could not find them. One evening, as he made his way back from yet another fruitless search, he saw a female figure standing only a few hundred yards from the tower. He rode towards her, dismounted and raced into her outstretched arms. She then took him by the hand and led him into a copse of trees nearby.

From then on he met her every day at the same time. At her insistence it had to be at the same place almost under the very walls of Littledean Tower. He was totally besotted. Soon however, the pair were spotted and news of the affair reached the ears of his wife, Margaret. She challenged her husband with his unfaithfulness and threw her wedding ring at him. She demanded to know who the woman was but he remained taciturn. A few days later the laird had to travel some distance on business. He left early in the morning and was not due to return until late at night. In the early evening one of Margaret's servants reported that she had spotted the woman entering the copse of trees. Determined to find out who her husband's lover was, Margaret rounded up a number of retainers and surrounded the small copse. They walked in and met in the middle but the copse was empty. The only thing they had seen was a hare that had darted through the line of retainers and scampered across the field. It was a tired and morose laird who made his way back to Littledean that night. As he rode along, he passed a hare standing by the side of the track. It seemed to be watching him intently. He rode on. When he glanced behind him, he was surprised but not alarmed to see that the hare seemed to be following him up the track. As he stared into the gathering gloom, he noticed another hare and then another until there was a whole pack of them following him. He urged his horse to go faster, but the hares drew closer until they had surrounded him. A cold sweat of fear broke out on him. He tried to crush them under his horse's hooves but they easily avoided the flailing of the panic-stricken animal. He took out his sword and slashed at them. He succeeded in cutting the paw of one of them who, bolder than the rest had leapt up on to his saddle. The wounded hare dropped off and limped away into the night following the rest of the pack. On looking around the laird discovered that he had ridden far from the road to Littledean and was close to the village of Midlem, a place reputed to be the home to many witches. It was a white-faced laird who arrived back at the tower. Shaking and muttering, "Devils! Devils!"

As he related the events of the night to his wife, he took off his pistol holster and to his astonishment and horror a severed human hand fell on the floor. It was a woman's hand. To his great consternation he saw that on one of its fingers was his wife's wedding ring. The last time he had seen the ring was when he had placed it on the finger of his mysterious, but passionate lover. He pierced the hand with his sword and hurried outside, mounted his horse and galloped off to a bank opposite a deep part of the Tweed into which he hurled the hand. As he made his way back, he recognized the small wood where he had first met his mysterious lover. He entered the cottage and saw the woman huddled by a fire with her back towards him. He reached out and grasped her by the shoulder. Slowly she turned around. It was an old woman who faced him. She was wrinkled and bony but deep in the hate-filled eyes glaring at him, he detected the woman who had ensnared him with her passion. She held out the raw, bleeding stump of her arm. She hissed at him that as he had taken it, he would never be parted from it. He stared at her, speechless with horror and then turned and raced back through the darkness to Littledean Tower.

When he arrived at the tower he refused all food and drink. He spent days sitting in front of the fire gazing morosely into the flames. The hand appeared from nowhere. He found it on the floor, picked it up and hurled it from the window. When he eventually retired to his bedroom, he found it underneath his pillow. He threw it into the fire and watched as it burned to a cinder.

The next morning passed with no sound coming from the bedchamber. By the afternoon his wife was so concerned that she ordered the servants to break down the door. They did so. When they entered the room the laird was lying dead in front of the cold embers of the fire. Marks on his throat indicated that he had been strangled.

It is claimed that on stormy nights the ghosts of the laird and his horse can still be seen galloping madly through the driving rain and screaming wind in the fields near Littledean Tower.

In later years the Kers of Littledean would appear to have become more respectable members of the Maxton community. James Ker, son of Ker of Littledean became minister of Abbotsrule parish. It was also said that the Kers of Littledean suffered greatly for their support of the Covenant. One of them was Margaret Ker, known as the 'Old Lady of Littledean.' In October, 1684 she stood before the court of Jedburgh accused of refusing to take the 'oath of allegiance' and of not attending her parish church services for two years. For these offences she was severely fined. It is not clear whether this Margaret Ker was the same old lady who was to haunt the tower for many years. Apparently in her lifetime she was very zealous in extracting her rents and dues from her hard-pressed tenants. She hid a great quantity of her cash in the tower but when she died her spirit repented of what she had done in her lifetime and could find no rest until she had atoned for her sins. Her apparition haunted the tower, frightening the inhabitants, looking for someone who would perform a good deed for her out of charity alone.

One evening a young serving maid was cleaning shoes in the kitchen. Glancing down she saw what she described as an 'elf-light' shining on the floor and gradually getting bigger and bigger. Suddenly it vanished and an old woman dressed in old fashioned clothing came in to the kitchen and asked if she could warm herself at the fire. The girl noticed that her shoes were wet and covered with mud and offered to clean them. The old lady then told her that a large sum of money was hidden in the bottom step of the main stair. The maid was to dig it out and give half of it to the laird and half to the poor of Maxton village. If this were done she would be able to sleep easy in her grave. The girl did as had been told and the ghost of the 'little old lady of Littledean' was never seen again.

On a bright summer day the tower of Littledean is a picturesque ruin. I had intended to visit it at night, particularly when it was stormy with lots of thunder and lightning, but so far I have not managed it.

Getting There

Littledean Tower is about 3 miles from the village of St Boswells. You follow the A699 road to Kelso, pass through Maxton village and about half a mile down the road you will see a sign on your left indicating Ploughlands farm. Follow the track until it turns sharply to the right. It would be advisable to park here if there is space. You should remember Ploughlands is a busy working farm and it would be courteous to ask permission to visit the site. The tower is in a corner of a field some way up the track. If the field has crops in it, you can walk around the edges. If you manage to get there you will be struck by what an impressive ruin it is. If the day is drawing to an end and it looks as if rain is coming on, those of a nervous disposition should be encouraged to make haste and leave!

Littledean Tower

The Haunted Road

It is a fairly unremarkable country road. There is nothing to suggest to the casual observer that it was here that occurred, what was later described by no less a body than the Society for Psychic Research as, *one of the best authenticated hauntings of modern times.*

Benrig road is on the immediate outskirts of the village of St Boswells. It leads to the old village burial ground, though there is no evidence that it is in any way linked with the series of events that took place here towards the end of the 19th century.

In the late afternoon of May 7th,1892, Miss Matilda Scott was making her way home along the Benrig road after having taken a solitary, Sabbath-day walk. Overcome by a sudden impulse to run, she sprinted to the top of a short incline, bordered on one side by a small plantation. She came to an abrupt halt, however, when she spotted a man, dressed all in black, walking in front of her. As she was a bit embarrassed about being seen running on the Sabbath, she waited awhile to let him get some distance in front of her. She watched as the man strode round the bend in front of her, though as she was on a small rise, she could still see him. All of a sudden he vanished like a puff of smoke blown away by the wind, only there was no wind, not even a breeze. Matilda was bewildered. There was no way the man could have left the road as it was bordered by a thick beech hedge. As she walked on and turned the bend, she saw her sister, Louisa, standing a little further down the road with a stricken expression on her face, *Where on earth did that man go who was walking beside you?* she asked Matilda. The two girls looked fearfully about them, but all they saw were quiet fields with a few disinterested cattle grazing in the late afternoon sun.

Later Louisa was to explain that she had seen a man, whom she thought was a clergyman, making his way towards her. One moment he was there and the next he was gone. Seconds later she saw Matilda running down the road and watched as she suddenly came to an abrupt halt and looked around, an expression of puzzlement on her face.

It would appear that the girls had seen the figure in roughly the same place, but at slightly different times - a fact that was to be of great interest to the Society for Psychic Research when they came to investigate the occurrence.

It was not the first reported sighting of a ghost on the Benrig road. About twenty years earlier a farmer had been driving his gig from Benrig to St Boswells village when he saw an elderly man walking some way ahead of him. He was dressed all in black l*ike a minister of the old time.* The farmer passed him and pulled up just in front of the plantation with the intention of offering the old man a lift. When he turned round the old man had disappeared.

In 1874 a nine-year-old girl had been making her way home to Benrig from St Boswells, when she too, saw an old man walking in front of her. She was particularly struck by the fact that the tails of his old-fashioned coat were flapping in the wind. When she turned the corner at the plantation the old man was nowhere to be seen.

Two months after the Scott sisters had their first encounter with the phantom stroller, Matilda and another sister, Susan, were walking along the same stretch of road when a figure dressed in black approached them in the near distance. Now Matilda was not exactly what you would call a shrinking violet. She was quite determined to get a closer look at this apparition, who had by now become the talk of the village. As she approached the walker, she took a good look at him. She noticed that: *He was dressed entirely in black, consisting of a long coat with gaiters ad knee breeches. His legs were very thin, and he wore a wide, white cravat around his throat, such as I have seen in old pictures. On his head was a low crown exceeding hat - the fashion I am unable to describe. His face, of which I saw only the profile, was exceedingly thin and deathly. As we were peering closely at the apparition, he faded away to the bank on our right.* They rushed to the spot where he had disappeared - but there was no sign of him.

A few months later the same two girls were picking strawberries from the bank at the top of the incline on the Benrig road when they heard what they described as a thudding sound behind them. The pair turned and were startled to see the ghost standing just behind staring intently at them. The girls were paralysed with fright at the expression on his white face which contrasted dramatically with black clothes. The sisters clung to each other, and watched with horror as the apparition started to dissolve in front of them. That was all too much and they were galvanised into action. They screamed and fled down into the village - their strawberries forgotten. A single glance backwards revealed the last wisps of the apparition floating like smoke in the air. In moments it had entirely gone.

Almost a year later Matilda was once again walking down the Benrig road in the early morning. She saw a dark figure walking ahead of her and, thinking it was a woman she knew, hurried to catch up with her. As Matilda got closer she realised that this was no village woman she was following and that once again she was seeing the apparition. With no hesitation the bold Matilda approached the figure, determined to get a look at what was already being referred to as *The Ghost of Benrig*. However, when she got within a few yards the figure seemed to skim away. All of a sudden it came to a halt and for the second time Matilda felt a cold chill of fear. Slowly the apparition turned around. *There he was gazing at me with a vacant expression and the same ghastly pallid features. He was dressed in black silk stockings and knee buckles, short knee breeches and a long black coat.* After a few moments he turned from her, floated away and seemed to evaporate into a mist a few yards in front of her. Within a few seconds the mist had dissipated and Matilda was alone. She resolved then and there never to walk on the Benrig road again unless she had a companion.

The next reported sighting of the phantom clergyman was over a year later on the 14th August 1894. A local governess, Miss Mary Irvine, was returning to her home at Crossflat, near St Boswells at about four o'clock in the afternoon. As she walked down the Benrig road she saw a man, *all dressed in black*, walking up and down in front of the small plantation. Two things struck her as being rather odd. She was intrigued by his quaint clothes: *His dress resembled that of a clergyman of a past generation.* He also appeared to be talking to a man who was cutting the hedge on the side of the road and who seemed to be completely ignoring the strange old man. As she approached to within a few yards of the pair, the old man suddenly vanished, silently and instantaneously. Mary's heart seemed to stop beating as a wave of fear swept through her. The hedge cutter went on working without once looking behind him. When Mary finally gathered her wits she walked on, having decided to say nothing to the hedge cutter who might think her deranged. She reached nearby Benrig House where she became quite hysterical.

By now the whole village and much of the surrounding area were aware of the ghostly reputation of the road and several more people claimed to have spotted the apparition. The lodge keeper at Lessudden House, the home of the Scott sisters, said that several years before Matilda's first encounter with the apparition, she had got *a terrible fright* when she saw a man dressed in black just down by the old graveyard. Another woman, who had been walking home at dusk from the nearby village of Maxton, spied a tall figure walking just ahead of her. When she was about to pass him she noticed that: *He was so light of foot he made no sound in walking.* She was so unnerved by this that she left the road and took off across the fields in order to reach her home as quickly as possible.

Matilda Scott was to see the apparition on three other occasions. In August 1898, when she was out walking with her sisters, she caught sight of him walking on the other side of the hedgerow and keeping pace with them. When they reached a gate in the field Matilda looked over, but the apparition had disappeared. She saw him again in July 1900 and once again the following month. He was standing beside a man with a pony and trap who was cutting the grass on the road verge. As she approached them, the apparition vanished. The grass cutter was rather bewildered and said that he had seen nothing. He did look around nervously and then confided in her that, *The road is not a safe place to one come down alone.* This was the last reported sighting of the Benrig ghost.

There was, of course, considerable speculation among the villagers as to the identity of the ghost. One story that gained a great deal of currency was that it was the ghost of a clergyman who had apparently murdered his servant one hundred and fifty years before. Unfortunately, as far as the credibility of this tale is concerned, the ministers of St Boswells are fairly well documented and there is nothing in the records to substantiate such a tale. In addition, the incumbent minister at the time alluded to was remarkable for the shortness of his stature, being only five feet tall. He hardly fits the description given by the many witnesses who saw the Benrig ghost. Nothing in the local records can provide any clues to the identity of the mysterious apparition who excited the interest of the local population for so long. Neither is there any indication of anything untoward being associated with that stretch of road.

The Society for Psychic Research was sufficiently intrigued to make a full report on the sightings and sent one of their investigators to St Boswells where he interviewed the principal witnesses. What particularly impressed him was the remarkable agreement about the general appearance and dress of the apparition as detailed by all of the witnesses. It was thought that the ghost could have been, *the result of a subtle influence in the locality visible only to those with a certain psychic sensitiveness.* Young Louisa Scott certainly declared that the apparition never appeared when she was consciously thinking about it.

The Benrig road is still a popular walk on a Sunday afternoon. The fact that the ghost has not been sighted for so long might suggest that the area has been secretly exorcised. Alternatively there could have been a sharp decrease in *psychic sensitivity* among the general population.

Or maybe the Sunday strollers are just not telling.

Getting There

The Benrig road is on the outskirts of the village of St Boswells. From the Edinburgh side of the A68 turn left just inside the village on the B6404. Carry on straight through the village. There is a sharp left bend and you come along a sign indicating the end of the 30mph limit. Turn up the road on your right. It is marked as leading to Benrig Cemetery. You are now on the Benrig road, you can see there is still a beech hedge. If you see rather skinny person dressed in old-fashioned clothes, don't stop to ask him the time

- the response could be quite unnerving!
At the end of the road you can turn left to Maxton (and Littledean Tower) or turn right taking you back to St. Boswells.

The Benrig Road

True Thomas

True Thomas lay on Huntlie Bank;
A ferlie he spied with his ee,
And there he saw a ladye bright,
Come riding down by the Eildon Tree. "

These well-known lines begin Sir Walter Scott's adaptation of an old ballad which tells the story of how Thomas the Rhymer met with the Queen of Elfland and lived with her in her underground domain for seven years. Before he returned to his home he had been given the power of looking into the future, but had to promise to go back to Elfland when the Queen summoned him. Eventually he received the summons and disappeared back to Elfland never to be seen on earth again.

Such is the basic matter of legend. Yet Thomas the Rhymer was not simply a figure of legend, he was a real person who lived the life of a small laird in Scottish Borderland of the 13th century. He remains, however, an elusive, mysterious figure who flits in and out of the pages of Scottish history in an ultimately infuriating way. Widely famed for the accuracy of his prophecies both during his lifetime and for many centuries after his death; his greatest importance may have been as a poet, writing in the vernacular almost a hundred years before Chaucer and who may well be regarded as the father of Scottish literature.

An early document describes him as *Thomas Rimor de Ercildun*; Er-cildun, from the Gaelic Arciol Dun, was situated at the west end of the present-day Berwickshire village of Earlston which lies thirty miles from Berwick on the river Leader, a northern tributary of the Tweed. It was a place of considerable importance in the 12th and 13th centuries, having strong links with the Earldom of March and with the Lindsey family. About a mile eastward from Ercildun was a castle, the residence of the Earl of March where King David the First probably signed the foundation chapter for Melrose Abbey. There still exists in the village an ivy-clad ruin known as The Rhymer's Tower that local tradition says was the home of Thomas. It is unlikely, however, that the present ruin existed in the 13th century though it would have been built on the site of an older construction. In the wall of the church at Earlston is a stone with the inscription:

> *Auld Rhymer's race,*
> *Lies in this place*

In 1782 the original inscription was defaced by a drunkard and the minister insisted on it being replaced. Unfortunately the defaced characters which were said to have been very ancient were replaced by more modern ones. The original stone was said to have come from an earlier church building.

Even his real name is in some doubt. He has come down to us as

Thomas the Rhymer. Early documents give his name as Thomas Rimor or Rymour. At first it was thought that this was a version of Rhymer reflecting his skills as a poet and versifier, but Rimour was a not uncommon name in Berwickshire in the 13th century. A *John Rhymou'*, a Berwickshire freeholder, is named as having paid homage to Edward the First in 1296. Several Scottish writers such as Blind Harry, the author of the early Scottish poem on the life of Sir William Wallace, refer to him as Thomas Rimour and it is likely that this was his actual surname. Traditionally, the Learmonts or Learmonths, who later owned Thomas' estates at Ercildoune, claimed descent from the Rhymer. Michael Lermontoff, the 19th century Russian poet, claimed to be a descendant through this link. Thomas certainly never used the name, Learmont, during his lifetime and it was the 16th century historian, Hector Boece, who first referred to him as Sir Thomas Learmont. Boece was not the most reliable of historians and there is no suggestion from any other source that Thomas was ever knighted. Surnames were, however, only starting to become fixed in lowland Scotland at this time. It could well be that Thomas, or one of his sons married an heiress named Learmont (the name could be a corruption of Leader-mount) and subsequently the family adopted the name. Like much else about this enigmatic character his real name is still a matter for conjecture.

His name appears in two contemporary documents. In one: *Thomas de Ercildun* appears as a witness to an agreement whereby Petrus de Haga de Bermersyde agreed to pay half a stone of wax annually to the abbot and convent of Melrose for the Chapel of St. Cuthbert. This document is undated but from analysis of the other signatories it would appear to be from the mid 13th century when Thomas would have been a comparatively young man. Possibly a more important document is the one dated the 2nd of November 1294. It is the record of a deed conveying the land held by Inheritance by *Thomas de Er-cildoun, son and heir of Thomas Rymour de Ercildoun* to the Trinity House of Soltra. This has usually been interpreted as the date of Thomas' death. However, it may be that the second-named Thomas was his father and that the son left his lands to the church and went into retirement. In Blind Harry's epic poem on Wallace, Thomas is linked with events in his hero's life that took place in Ayr in 1296/97. The poet says:

Thomas Rimour in to the Faile was then.

The Faile or Feale was a monastery of the Trinitarian Red Friars located just outside Ayr. These were troubled times for Scotland and it is not hard to imagine the scholarly and elderly Thomas deciding to spend his last days, sequestered from the uproar caused by the English occupation, within the tranquil walls of a monastery. We can only surmise, however, for these brief and tantalising glimpses of Thomas the Rhymer reveal little of the man whose life remains shrouded in mystery.

Whatever mystery surrounds the actual life of Thomas, there is no doubt about the reputation as a seer that he developed during his lifetime and which grew rapidly after his death. The basis for this reputation lies in his prediction of the death of King Alexander III in 1285. According to the historian, Walter Bower who died in 1449, Thomas was visiting Patrick, the Earl of March, in his castle of Dunbar. The Earl asked Thomas what the weather would be like the next day. Thomas' reply was: *"That, before the next day at noon, such a tempest should blow as Scotland had not felt for many years before."* The next day noon came and went with no sign of a storm. Thomas' weather prediction, it would appear, had been somewhat inaccurate. Shortly afterwards a messenger arrived bringing news of the death of the king. During a storm he had plunged to his death over the cliffs at Kinghorn in Fife. It was a calamity that was to see the start of the long struggle with England. It also established Thomas' reputation as a seer, for the tale spread quickly and no doubt was somewhat enlarged in the telling.

Thomas may have started out with something of a reputation as a predictor of weather, a not unimportant ability in these days; but in an age when the supernatural was as real as everyday life, he soon came to be regarded with some awe as being no canny. His fame as a seer quickly spread and became proverbial after his death. An early writer stated that: *This Thomas was one man of great admiration to the people, and schaw sundry things as they fell; howbeit they were ay hid under obscure wordis.* His prophecies were first gathered together and published in the early 17th century. It is now almost impossible to establish which of them were contemporary with Thomas and which were later additions and forgeries. The problem with prophetic utterances, particularly when they are obscurely worded, is that they will fulfil themselves if people really want them to. There was also a tendency for prophecies to be ascribed to Thomas at a later date in order to fit the circumstances of current times and future expectations. However sceptical we may be, though, about his supposed prophecies, what cannot be denied is the veneration he received as a seer from the great mass of the people. So much so that future forgers felt they had to put

Thomas' name to their works in order to give them credibility.

An interesting aspect of the prophecies is the possible light they may shed on Thomas' life. An analysis of the places associated with Thomas the Rhymer shows a remarkable number linked with the northeast and Angus. An example of this comes from the parish of Old Deer in Aberdeenshire. According to the story, which was written down about 1732, there was a place called Cummin's Craig at Aikey brae in the parish. It was at this spot that one of the Cummins, an Earl of Buchan who lived at the time of Alexander III, fell from his horse and was killed.

Apparently the Earl had called Thomas, Thomas the Lyar to show how little he thought of his predictions. Thomas denounced the Earl in the following words, which needless to say were fulfilled to the letter

Tho' Thomas the Lyar thou call 'st me
A sooth tale I shall tell to thee:
By Aikey side they horse shall ride,
He shall stumble and thou shalt fa'
Thy neck bone shall break in twa
And dogs shall thy bones gnaw
And, maugre all thy kin and thee,
Thy own belt thy bier shall be."

It was about this time that the Gordon family, who came from Berwickshire, and whose lands neighboured Ercildoune, were starting to settle in the north-east, a process that was to eventually make them the dominant family there. Given the many associations with Thomas the Rhymer in that part of Scotland, it is likely that Thomas spent some time there rather than in Elfland, where his

Borderland contempories thought he had gone.

Although Thomas is popularly remembered for his prophecies, his main claim to historical fame lies in the authorship of the poem *Sir Tristram* - the first rendering into English of the classic tale of *Tristram and Isolde*. It had been assumed lost until a copy was discovered in the Advocate's Library in Edinburgh in the early years of last century. It is a 3000-line poem with stanzas of 11 lines and is written in the language of 13th century lowland Scotland and northern England. There has been some controversy regarding the authorship of the poem which underwent a number of changes when it was taken up by the troubadours of medieval France. Undergoing several translations and alterations, what is original and what has been plagiarized has been a matter for considerable scholarly debate. However, Robert Manning of Brunne, a contemporary of Thomas, stated that Thomas of Ercildune was the author of Sir Tristram.

Certainly the local people in the Borders regarded Thomas as a great poet as well as a seer. It was not uncommon for particularly clever men who were poets to be possessed of magical powers in an age when few were literate. Poems have been ascribed to others on less evidence than we have for Thomas' claim to the authorship of Sir Tristram. He certainly received the endorsement of Sir Walter Scott who referred to him as *the father of Scottish literature.*

The ballad, adapted by Sir Walter Scott, which was to make Thomas a figure of legend was written no earlier than 1400 or one hundred years after Thomas' death. The skeleton of the story actually pre-dates Thomas' life, having its origins in Brythonic

Welsh tradition. Thomas was probably made the hero of an old story at some point after his death. It is this tale, beautifully told by Sir Walter Scott, that placed Thomas of Ercildoun firmly within the ranks of legend rather than history. After spending seven years in faery land, Thomas returns with the gift of prophecy. Before leaving the underground realm he had to promise to return at the summons of the Queen. One evening, as he was carousing at home with friends, a snow-white hart and a hind came out of the forest and walked quietly through the village streets. Thomas recognized the summons from his Queen. He left his home, went into the forest and was never seen again.

Another local tradition says that Thomas was murdered on the path through the woods to Thirlestane castle where he was going. His death, like his life, remains a mystery. He may have retired and died in an Ayrshire monastery or have been assassinated in a Berwickshire wood. Whatever the case the legend was accurate when it says:

> *Some said to the hill, and some to the glen,*
> *The wondrous course had been;*
> *But ne'er in haunts of living men*
> *Again was Thomas seen*

Getting There

Earlston is on the A68, but the main part of the village runs up Main Street to the east from the junction with the A68. The church with the Rhymer inscription is at the east end of the village.

Index

Aberdeenshire; 180
Abbotsrule; 164
Alba; 21,22,23
Alexander II; 28
Alexander III; 178,180
Almond, river; 23
Aneirin; 48
Adomman; 51
Allanbank; 62,63,64,65,66
Allanton; 66
Angus; 98,180
Arderydd, Battle of; 50,51,54
Armstrongs; 93,98,99,100
Arthur, King; 46,145
Arthuret Knowes; 51
Auchencrow; 153
Auld, Agnes; 69
Australia; 7
Ayr; 178
Ayrshire; 49,50,105,182

Bertha of Badlieu'; 23,24,25,26
Badlieu; 8,20,22,24,25,26
Baillie of Jerviswoode; 30
Balliol, Edward; 91
Bathgate, Elizabeth; 152
Benrig; 167,168,169,170,171,173,174
Bermersyde; 177
Berwick-upon-Tweed; 20,32,176
Berwickshire; 13,27,62,63,64,67,152, 154,176,177,180,182
Berwickshire Naturalists Society; 35
Blackadder, river; 62,65
Blackadder, Jenny; 65
Blackadder, Thomas; 65
Blacksmill; 70
Blind Harry; 178
Blyndley; 38
Boece, Hector; 177

De Bolebek; 85
Bonchester Bridge; 18
Bonchester Hill; 17
Bosworth, Battle of; 47
Bowden Moor Reservoir; 146
Bower, Walter; 178
Branxholm; 112
Branxholm, Laird of; 88,89
Britons; 22,46,50,143
Broadlaw; 20
Bruce, Captain; 40
Bruce, Edward; 87
Bruce, King Robert; 87,89,98
Buccleuch, Duke of; 90,94,
Buchan, Earl of; 180
Buckholm Tower; 37,38,40,41,43,44
Burns, Robert; 105,106,111

Caerlaverock; 50
Caesar, Julius; 141
Calder, George; 34
Calder, Robert McLean; 34
Caledon, wood of; 23,26,53
Calvin, John; 149
Canonbie Dick; 144,145
Carlisle; 49,50,112
Carnwath; 55
Carterhaugh; 115,116,117,118,124
Carwinelow; 51
Castletown; 86,87,95
Catterick; 48
Cavers; 108
Caxton, William; 46
Charles II; 38,39
Chaucer; 176
Cheviots; 125
Child, Francis J; 114

183

Chirnside; 66
Chirnside, Isobel; 69
Choicelea farm; 74
Coel Hen; 50
Coldingham; 153
Columba, St.; 49,51
Constantine, king; 21,23
Core; 20
Cornwall; 45
Corwhinley; 50
Cout of Keilder; 87,88
Crailinghall; 111,112
Crochallan Fencibles; 106
Crozier; 98
Cunningham, Allan; 107,109

Dacre, Lord; 92
Dalriada; 54
David I; 85,176
Davidson, Rev. Henry; 42,43
Dawston; 53
Deans, Mrs; 73
Dere Street; 77
Dirrington Law; 70
Donaldson, William; 152
Douglas; 59,92
Douglas, Earl Archibald; 92
Douglas, Jean; 59,60
Douglas-Hamilton, Anne; 59
Douglas, Sir William; 91
Druids; 141
Duff, king; 2_
Duncan, king; 25
Dundalk, battle of; 87
Duns; 35,66,74
Durie, John, of Grange; 40
Drumelzier Church; 45,53,55
Dumbarton; 49,51,89,98
Dun, John; 69
Dunbar; 178

Earlston; 176,180,182
Eckford; 42
Edgar, Elizabeth; 14
Edgar, Rev. Nicol;10,11,12,13,14, 15,16,17,18
Edgar, Susannah; 14
Edict of Nantes; 32
Edinburgh; 43,48,63,64,79,88,106, 132,154,155,156,173
Edward III; 92
Eildon Hills; 139,140,141,142,143, 144,145,146
Elder, Madge; 32
Ellet; 98
Elliot, Gavin;102
Elliot, Geordie; 40
Elliot, George; 40,41
Elliot, Gilbert; 102,108,110
Elliot, Isobel; 41
Elliot, Jock, of the Park; 93
Elliot, Robert, of Redheugh; 102
Elliots; 93,94,97,98,99,100,101, 102,110,111
Esk, river; 51
Ettrick Forest; 92
Ettrick river; 117,118
Eyemouth; 151,152

Falnash, Archibald Elliot of; 109,112
Floors Castle; 71
Forfar; 98
Fortrui; 22,24
Foul Ford; 67,71,72,73,74,75
Fraser, Sir Simon; 58
Fraziers; 58
Fruid; 20

Gala Water; 38
Galashiels; 37,38,42,43,44
Galloway; 50

Geoffrey of Monmouth; 45,46,47,49,53
Gilmour, Sir John; 64
Girvan, Margaret; 153
Glasgow; 51
Glasgow, Archbishop of; 93
Glastonbury; 45
Glencoe; 14
Gododdin; 48,49
Gordons; 180
Greenlaw; 35,67,69,70,71,74
Greenlaw Moor; 67,70
Gruoch; 25
Gwendollau; 49,50,51,52

Haddington; 85
Hamilton, Alexander; 153,154
Hart Fell; 20
Hawick; 17,91,95,112
Hays; 58
Henderson, Tom; 80
Henderson, William; 108,109,110,111,112
Henry II; 46
Henry III; 86
Hepburn, Francis; 94
Hepburn, James, Earl of Bothwell; 93,94
Hepburn, Patrick, Earl of Bothwell; 92
Herdmanston; 28,29
Hermitage Castle; 8,84,85,86,87, 88,89, 90,92,93,94,95,97,98,103
Hermitage river; 86
Hobkirk; 11,12,13,14,15,17,18
Hobkirk Church; 10,12,17,18
Home, Sir George; 154,155
Home, Lady; 154,155
Home, Margaret; 152
Home, Sir Alexander, of Renton; 152
Homer; 48

Hop-Pringle, Johne; 38
Hop-Pringle; 37 Huguenots; 32
Humber,river; 49
Hume, George; 28,29
Hume, Grizell; 31,32
Hume, Patrick; 28,29
Hume, Sir Patrick; 30,31
Humes; 28

Iona; 25
Irvine, Mary; 171

James I; 90
Jed, river; 77,81,83
James VI; 94,150
Jedburgh; 12,77,78,79,80,81,82,83, 93,94,107, 108,110,111,126,155
Jedburgh Abbey; 77,80,128
Johnstoun, Patrick;81,82

Kelso; 67,130,165
Kelso Abbey; 128,143
Kenneth III; 21,23,24,25
Kentigern(Mungo), St.; 27,49,50,51,53
Ker, Margaret; 164
Kers of Cessford; 158
Kers of Littledean; 163,164
Ker, James; 164
Kidd, Helen; 100,101,102,103
Kidd's Tower; 96,103
Kinghorn; 179
Knout, Sir Richard; 88

Ladhope Moor; 40
Lammas Fair; 16
Lammermuir Hills; 29,48,67,68,74
Langshaw; 44
Lang, Andrew, 5
Larriston; 10,31,126
Larriston, Elliot of; 100
Lauder; 150,151

Lawson, Meg; 155,156
Leader, river; 176
Learmont name; 177
Lermontoff, Michael;177
Lessudden House; 171
Liddell Crags; 86,95
Liddell, John; 13
Liddell, river; 51,86,96,97,103
Liddesdale; 54,85,86,87,91,92,93,94, 97,98,99, 100,101,102
Lindsey family; 176
Linton; 125,126,127,128,129,130
Littledean Tower; 8,157,158,159, 160,161,162,163,164,165,174
Lomond, Loch; 49
Longformacus; 68,69,70,71,74
Longtown; 50,52
Lukup, John; 156
Lunham, Janet; 69

Macbeth; 25
Macgabrain, Aiden' 53
Malcolm II; 25
Malcolm IV; 77
Malory, Sir Thomas; 46,47
Manderston; 154
Mangerton, Laird of; 88
Manning, Robert, of Brunne; 181
March, Earl of, Patrick; 178
March, Earl of, William Douglas; 58,59
Marchmont House; 32
Marchmont, Earl of; 32
Margaret, Maid of Norway; 87
Mary, Queen of Scots; 93,94
Maxton; 157,158,164,165,171,174
McEwan family; 28
McGill, Rev. Walter; 110
Meldedus; 53.
Melrose; 40,91,128,142,144,146,177
Melrose Abbey; 42,176
Merlin; 45,46,47,49,52,53,54,55

Merse; 68
Michie, John; 72
Midlem; 162
Moffat; 26
Monivaird; 25
Montrose, Duke of; 39
Moray; 25
Morebattle; 125,130
Mungo's, St, Fair; 28,30

Neidpath Tower; 56,57,58,59
Neville, Ralph; 91
Newark Tower; 117
Newcastleton; 95,102
Newmill; 109,112
Newtown St. Boswells; 146
Niel family; 68,69,74
Niel, Francis; 69
Niel, Henry; 71,72,73
Niel, John; 69,70,71,73
Niel, Robert; 69,74
Niell, John; 153,154,155
Nine Stane Rig; 86,89,95
Ninian, St; 49
Nixons; 98
Normans; 85,86,126
Norsemen; 21,128,129
North Berwick; 150
Northamptonshire; 85

Old Deer; 80
Ord, Rev. Selby; 70,73
Oxnam Water; 109,110

Packman's Brae; 30,36
Pearlin Jean; 61,62,63,64,65,66
Peebles; 55,58,60
Perthshire; 22,23,25
Philiphaugh, battle of; 39
Picts; 22,48
Pinkerton, Nell; 80
Ploughlands Farm; 165

Polmood; 23,24
Polwarth; 27,28,29,32,33,34,35,36
Polwarth Church; 30,31,36
Polwarth, Elizabeth de; 28
Polwarth, Sir Patrick de; 28
Powsail Burn; 53,55
Pringle, George, 39,40,41,42
Pringle, James; 39
Pringles; 37,38,39

Queensberry, Duke of; 58,59

Rae, Alexander; 151
Ramsay, Alan; 29
Ramsay, Sir Alexander; 91
Redbraes Castle; 31,32
Redheugh; 98
Redpath, Adam; 72
Rheged; 49
Richard III; 47
Richardson, James; 71
Ringan, Red; 88,89,90
Romans; 77,141,142
Roxburgh Castle; 91
Roxburghshire;125
Ruglen, Earl of; 59
Rule Valley; 12,17
Rydderich Hael; 50,51,52,53

Saltoun; 86
Scots; 22
Scott, Jean; 102
Scott, John, of Spottiswoode; 73
Scott, Louisa; 168,173
Scott, Matlida;
167,168,169,170,171,172
Scott, Susan; 169
Scott, Sir Walter;
57,90,97,109,115,127,
139,175,181,182
Scott, Sir Walter, of Branxholme; 94
Scott, Walter, of Tushielaw; 59,60

Selgovae; 77
Selkirk; 5,26,39,116,117,131,132,
133,137,138, 155,156
Selkirkshire; 115,117
Shortreed, Margaret; 82
Sinclair, Margaret; 28,29
Sinclair, Marion; 28,29
Sinclair, Sir John; 28,30
Sinclair, Sir William; 28
Sinclairs; 28
Solway Firth; 49
Somerset; 45
Somerville, John; 127
Somerville, Roger; 127
Somervilles; 128
De Soulis; 85,86,87,98
De Soulis, John; 87
De Soulis, Nicholas; 87
De Soulis, Ranulph; 86,87,89,90
De Soulis, William; 87,88,89,90,98
Southdean; 12
Spens, Patrick, of Kilspindie; 92
Spinnie, Meg; 80
Spottiswoode; 72
Sprott, George; 151
St. Boswells; 146,165,167,169,171,
173,174
St. George; 128
Stobs, Elliots of: 101,110
Strathclyde; 21,51,53
Stuart, Prince Charles Edward; 83
Stuart, Robert; 62.63,64
Sue Ryder Home; 32

Taliesin; 48
Talla; 20
Tam Lin; 114,115,116,117,118,119,
120,121,122,123,124
Tennyson; 47
Teviot, river; 108
Teviotdale; 91,107,109,111
Thirlstane Castle; 182

Thomas the Rymer; 143,144,
145,146,175,176,177,178,179,
180,181,182
Tintagel; 45
Torwoodlee; 38,39
Traprain Law; 140
Trimontium; 142
Tudor, Henry; 47
Turnbull; 11,12
Tweed, river; 20,22,26,45,49,
53,55,58,68,158, 163,176
Tweedmouth; 153
Tweedsmuir; 19,20,21,22,23,26
Tweeds Well; 18,26

Veitch, William; 13
Vortigen,King; 46
Votadini; 142

Walter the Bold; 89
Wedderburn; 28
Wedderlie, 13,17
Westruther; 13,67,74
Whitadder, river; 68
William of Orange; 31
Wilson, Robert; 70

Yarrow river; 117
Yetholm; 130